GW00374349

COSMIC!

NORTH LONDON

Edited by Simon Harwin

First published in Great Britain in 1998 by
POETRY NOW YOUNG WRITERS
1-2 Wainman Road, Woodston,
Peterborough, PE2 7BU
Telephone (01733) 230748

HB ISBN 0 75430 141 9
SB ISBN 0 75430 142 7

FOREWORD

With over 63,000 entries for this year's Cosmic competition, it has proved to be our most demanding editing year to date.

We were, however, helped immensely by the fantastic standard of entries we received, and, on behalf of the Young Writers team, thank you.

The Cosmic series is a tremendous reflection on the writing abilities of 8-11 year old children, and the teachers who have encouraged them must take a great deal of credit.

We hope that you enjoy reading *Cosmic North London* and that you are impressed with the variety of poems and style with which they are written, giving an insight into the minds of young children and what they think about the world today.

CONTENTS

Nicholas Sowemimo	38
Bobby Morris	39
Jordan Lewis	40
Jamie Cohen	40
Chase Burns	41
Nicholas Voegt	42
Ladi Lampejo	42
Adam Simmonds	43
Tom McAdam	44
Simon Malone	45
Ben Jacobs	46
Johnny Dart	47
Sam Wild	48
Alexander Taylor	49
Harry Blaiberg	49
Alex Miller	50
Hamish Edgar	50
Luke Vignali	51
Basil Yannakoudakis	51
Tristram Bainbridge	52
Marcus Schofield	53
Abdulla Mashaal	54
Charles Franklin	54
Patrick Rowlands	55
Joshua Bicknell	56
Alexander Manby	56
Stewart Allan	57
Adam Klug	58
Dheeraj Harjani	59
Alex Dodds	60
Robert Anderson	61
James Ridgway	62
Nicholas Baker	63

Muswell Hill Junior School

Celia Turnbull	63
Emma Bergamin-Davys	64
Harry Collins	64

North Harringay Junior School

Queenswell Junior School

THE POEMS

SPRING

Winter has passed,
It's springtime
Flowers start to bloom
I look out of my room
At the beautiful sunshine.
All the birds are singing
And the day is just beginning.
I hear the doorbell ringing
And all my friends are singing
'Come outside and play' they say
We all play in the park
And have so much fun
Because springtime has just begun.

Safia Altamash (10)
Craven Park Primary School

MUM COMMANDS

Brush your teeth, comb your hair
before you get to school.
After school do the dishes,
don't forget to feed the fishes.
Feed the cat, walk the dog
when you're finished feed the frog.
Empty your dustbin clean your room
hurry up 'cause dinner's soon.

Natasha McIntosh (10)
Craven Park Primary School

DAD'S WISH

As I go down memory lane
I can see where I went wrong,
I did not think of others as I went along.
I got in so much trouble but now those days are gone.

I have found that doing good is the right thing to do,
God do you know I am doing this for you
But I wish I was a boy again.

God is helping me in a special way
I listen to him every day
Now I know where I start,
You are forever in *my heart.*

Danny Joe Migliorini (10)
Drayton Park Primary School

FEELINGS

I feel like I'm in an elephant's trunk,
I feel like I'm very drunk.
I feel like I'm a train with no rails,
I feel like a finger without a nail.
I feel like a shark without a fin,
I feel like a very clean bin.
I feel like a pencil with no lead,
I feel like a duvet with no bed.
I feel like a tape player with no tape,
I feel like Batman with no cape.
I feel like an empty book,
I feel like I'm a companion to Captain Hook.

Robert Wiesner (10)
Drayton Park Primary School

WEIRD FEELINGS

I feel like daffodils on Mars,
I feel like rainbow beams in jars.
I feel like Land Rovers in pink guts,
I feel like dinosaurs in illuminated huts.
I feel like pollen in Chinese iguanas,
I feel as squashy as glowing bananas.
I feel like a car in chalk,
I feel like a marble in a hawk.
I feel like a spiral in a pencil,
I feel like a bed on a stencil.
When I go in the shade,
All these feelings start to fade.
When I go right in the sun,
Everything just turns to fun.

Zaki Rafiq-Khatana (9)
Drayton Park Primary School

FUNKY FLY

As scary as a monster, with an extra long tail,
As tasty as a hamburger stuffed with peas and quail.
As ugly as a Scottish lobster with a pierced nose,
As pretty as a black widow sitting on a rose,
As frightened as a prawn, eating frogspawn.
As horrible as a glass eye when it's stuck in kidney pie.
As funky as a fly when it's flying high,
As annoying as a bee that's buzzing around me,
As pretty as an ox when it's got the chicken pox.

Rowena Crowley (10)
Drayton Park Primary School

THE SLITHERING SNAKE

There was once a slithery snake,
who slithered by the lake,
he slithered till late at night,
he gave the humans a very big fright.

His daily meal wasn't nice,
he ate the humans' head-lice,
one day he got very cross
because his home grew loads of moss.

He'd cry and cry and cry and cry,
until he thought one day he'd die,
he lay down slowly one night yawning,
and sadly didn't get up in the morning.

After that the jungle was sad,
and everyone was very mad,
their memories were so nice and sweet,
they missed him massaging their feet!

Sally Burrows (10)
Drayton Park Primary School

LISTENING

Gloomy and dark
Shadows are faint
A little bit of light coming through the window plate.
I can hear some voices coming through the door,
They're scary, they're demon, there is someone coming
Through the floor.
Now everything has gone silent and very still
There is a little bit of light coming through the window-sill.

Yasmine Tabatabai (10)
Drayton Park Primary School

MOTHER NATURE

I see the birds chirping,
And flying from tree to tree,
Chirping their happy song for me.

I see trees swaying from side to side,
And the leaves growing,
Also the moss on the north side.

I see squirrels running around,
And I hear them making more,
More than one sound.

In the morning,
I see dew on the grass,
The wind blowing them from time to time,
This happens on and with the grass.

The lawn is being mown,
But don't run over,
A four-leaf clover.

The sun sets,
The moon rises,
In the dark come more surprises.

Nii Nartey (10)
Eldon Junior School

THE CHIMPS

Oh the lions were growling,
The tigers were prowling,
The zebras kept quietly grazing,
Kangaroos were all jumpy,
But the chimps were really amazing.

We heard rattlesnakes rattle,
Saw huge hairy cattle,
And land crabs, lobsters and shrimps.
There were penguins like waiters,
And great alligators,
But we kept going back to the chimps.

There were dolphins and seals,
A stingray, some eels,
And polar bears white as snow.
But the chimps were our aces,
Their habits and faces,
Were just like some people we know.

Michelle Chapman (10)
Eldon Junior School

THE SKY

T housands of birds fly all day,
H undreds of birds peck away,
E normous sets of stars at night make the
          sky really bright,
S unny sunset in the sky,
K ites flying up high,
Y ellow sunset shining bright like a
          star at night.

Maria Willett (10)
Eldon Junior School

6

THE GHOST TEACHER

The school is closed, the children gone,
But the ghost of the teacher lingers on.
She stands in the classroom, as clear as glass,
And calls the names of her absent class.
The school is shut, the children grown,
But the ghost of the teacher, all alone.
She puts the date on the board and floats about,
As the night goes on and the stars come out.
Between the desks - a glow in the gloom,
She calls for quiet in the noisy room.
As the moon comes up and the first owls glide,
She puts on her coat and steps outside.

In the moonlit playground, she's shadow free,
She stands on duty with a cup of tea.
As the night creeps up to the edge of the day,
She tidies all the plasticine away.
She utters the words that no one hears,
Picks up her bag and . . . disappears.

Zainab Danjuma (8)
Eldon Junior School

SPARKLING RAIN

Sparkling rain is lashing down,
Splishing sploshing down on my crown,
I'm not worried because I like rain,
Winter is my favourite season because it rains,
On rainy days I feel cold and wet,
I come in the house dripping wet,
My mum goes mad but I don't care
Because I like rain.

Stephanie Patel (9)
Eldon Junior School

LOVE IS AS RED AS RUBY

Your love is so devoted to me,
Your love is ever so hard to find,
Your love is something I will never forget,
Your love is like a ruby to me for,
I will keep it forever more,
Your beauty is like a ruby
For you are perfect to me.
This poem goes towards you
For your passion and tenderness
Will always keep me warm.

Choymei Chan (11)
Eldon Junior School

RAINFOREST

R ain is gently falling on the canopy,
A nimals running to find shelter,
I   nsects flying to save their lives,
N oisy stampedes running from thunder,
F or they think it is a hunter.
O ne may die or one may survive,
R esting for it will be a long night.
E verything is quiet,
S o everything is still except
T he trees rattling swiftly in the air.

Fatima Hamit (11)
Eldon Junior School

SUNSET

The sun disappeared beyond the crystal blue sea,
the sea looked so pure it looked like 100 diamond rings.

The sea was shining and glittering in the dark filled sky,
it twinkled like the stars sparkle in the sky.

The sun goes down peacefully and silently in the wide, blue sky.
The seagulls sing like nature's around. The sun is down.

Anthony Michael (10)
Eldon Junior School

WHEN I WAS BRAVE AND I WAS BOLD

When I played for my team I was the best they'd ever seen.

See me dribble see me pass
watch me move across the grass.
I was fast and I was stunning and I was brilliant at running.

I could score ten goals a game
every match would be the same
Shots from near shots from far,
headers, backheels, *what a star!*

Fans would shout for their hero, when I'd made a fifteen zero!

Sarah Hicks (10)
Garfield Primary School

FLYING

Peaceful, warm, summer's day,
Flying over a diamond blue sea,
Boats and ships racing along,
Cheerful people playing with the sand,
Everything so calm.

The basket tilting from side to side,
Making the world go round and round,
The hot air rising to the roof of the sphere balloon,
The heat making me feel dreamy and sleepy.

In front of me the sun slowly ascending to the horizon,
The balloon floating through the fluffy cloud,
As it continues its infinite journey.

Vikki Kothari (11)
Garfield Primary School

MY NEW SCHOOL BAG POEM

My school bag is blue,
Some parts are stuck together with glue.
It has some black parts,
but it has no hearts.
It has one zip,
I will tell you where to get it from, that's a tip.
It didn't cost much, but it's nice to touch.
My mum bought it for me,
And it's made me really happy.

Angela Lee (10)
Garfield Primary School

FLYING

Sun setting on the horizon,
The blue sky reaching down so low,
An expanse of blue sea down below
Invigorating and engulfing me,
And it ascends so very slow.

Silently, swooping, swaying and swishing,
Swiftly floating both low and high,
Gliding gently and gracefully,
Rocking and tilting saying good-bye.

The world seems to be moving below,
Hovering just like a hovercraft,
The beauty of the earth blow,
From all that can be seen from a raft.

Soon the hot air balloon glides,
And drifts away,
Before slowly descending,
And landing at bay.

Dilan Shah (10)
Garfield Primary School

GOOD AND EVIL

Good, evil, happy, sad.
Everyone is good in their own way even people which are mad.
Having an evil feeling about someone is bad, you can make them
very sad.
Being happy is great even better when you have a mate.
Evil people think they are cool but even an elderly person would
think they were a fool.

Isheeta Gor (9)
Garfield Primary School

WATER

Rain is trickling down the hillside,
As it forms minute dribbling streams,
Down they go meeting together,
Or maybe it just seems.

Meandering through the blue rivers,
Splashing past the rocks,
Soon it will find its destination,
But now it's only reached the loch.

Passing the rocks and still in the river,
It finally reaches the sea,
And when the sun comes up it will
                              evaporate,
You will see.

Jaysal Darjee (10)
Garfield Primary School

MONTHS, SEASONS

Life changes but you don't realise,
Time goes past and we get bigger.
The weather changes, autumn, winter, summer and spring
The months go past, the leaves are brown.
The sun goes past, the snow comes back.
The snow goes past the clouds are back.
The flowers are here so happy we are.

Maria Fernanda Garces (9)
Garfield Primary School

THE JOURNEY

Sad, lonely, terrified.
Dark, dingy, mystified.
Trying not to look back,
And face my sorrow.
I walk into the dark, dense forest,
As sad as can be.
Jumping on stepping stones
Alligators snapping at my feet.
Sick, sad, stressed
Climbing up the cliffs that grind in my soul.
Jagged rocks pierce my skin.
Ow! painful.
My heart beating, racing.
Over the cliffs not far away.
Is a village which looks bright and gay.
Tunnelling through a rabbit hole.
Slithering, sliding, squeezing through.
Swimming through the lake.
So close to home.
I may just give up.
No! I must keep on.
The journey can't be long.
So close to home.
I'm there.
I'll start a new leaf.

Remiah Cobbson (11)
Garfield Primary School

JACK FROST

Look out! Look out!
Jack Frost is about,
He's after your fingers and toes;
And all through the night
The gay little sprite
Is working, where, nobody knows.

He'll climb each tree
So nimble is he,
His silver powder he'll shake,
To windows he'll creep,
And while we're asleep,
Such wonderful pictures he'll make.

Across the grass
He'll merrily pass,
And change all the greenness -
To white,
Then home he'll go,
And laugh, 'Ho! Ho! Ho!
What fun I have had -
In the night.'

Kashfia Mariam (9)
Garfield Primary School

SPICE UP YOUR WORLD

S is for those spicy Spice Girls
P is for planet pop
I   is for ice-cool, so just chill
C is for cute people
E is for enjoying yourself

G is for *Girl Power*!
I is for innocent people
R is for red roses
L is for lovely days
S is for spice world!

Samira Jaali (10)
Garfield Primary School

COMPLAINING

I didn't do it so don't look at me,
Well OK then, but I only had three,
It's not that much, can't you see,
Why does everyone blame it on me?

Leave me alone, I've got enough on my plate,
I can't sing a song, and I can't get a date,
And, my best friend's left me for a new mate,
Why does everything have to happen to me?

My sister's being a pain and, she won't let me watch TV,
There's a lot of good shows now, on the BBC,
But it's no use because the good shows aren't for me
Why can't I watch TV?

I haven't tidied my room, and my grandma's gone berserk,
I'm really worried because, my mum's not back from work,
And my cousin's taken my bunny, oh, what a jerk,
Why does everyone keep annoying me?

Rozeta Sahota (10)
Garfield Primary School

I Know A Witch

I know a witch,
She lives next door,
She has a broomstick and a wand
She has rotten teeth,
And warts all over her face.

I wonder what she is doing
I ask myself
What she is doing with her black cat
On Hallowe'en Night.

I think she might be making a spell,
Or,
She might be scaring people on Hallowe'en Night
Or
She might be turning my teacher into a toad,
Or,
She might by flying past the moon.

I know a witch, she lives next door.

Jaimine Shah (10)
Garfield Primary School

My Teacher

My teacher is like a ball, bouncy, colourful,
But smooth and gentle, like silk,
Funny but serious at times,
She's a rainbow colourful and bright,
A warm gentle breeze,
A teddy to comfort you.

Richard Ibrahim (10)
Garfield Primary School

FLYING

The horizon descending below the sky line,
The graceful, silent, calm sky shining as bright as can be,
Stars begin to scamper amongst the moonlit sky,
Birds swooping,
Imaginary.

The light lit city below,
Shimmering so bright,
Like a candlelit table,
Gracefully swishing,
Staring at the moonlit lake,
Dreaming.

Swish, sway, swoosh, the light breeze,
So silent up above,
Gentle birds swoop playfully,
The city shining so bright below,
Peaceful.

Paul Reading (10)
Garfield Primary School

MY TEACHER

My teacher is like a soft piece of cake,
She is very funny but quiet as a mouse,
Like when she's very angry,
She looks sternly at your face,
But then she takes you out to play,
She's a very happy, good teacher,
A wonderful Arsenal mad supporter,
A very angry, funny, mad teacher.

Janak Tailor (11)
Garfield Primary School

PLANES

If you ever feel grim hop on a plane
Go to the nicest place on earth
It could be the USA or maybe Spain
You can travel in style or just regular
But you'll always feel great.

If you ever feel sad and low
Just put your headphones on
And listen to your favourite band
Or would you watch a blockbuster movie?
Get there quick and you won't feel sick.

When you arrive, you'll feel good inside
And have a great time!

Robbie Jones (9)
Garfield Primary School

WHISTLING

Oh, I can laugh and I can sing
And I can scream and shout,
But when I try to whistle,
The whistle won't come out.

I shape my lips the proper way,
I make them small and round,
But when I blow, just air comes out,
There is no whistling sound.

But I will keep trying very hard
To whistle loud and clear,
And some day soon I will be able to
Whistle tunes for everyone to hear.

Nishma Shah (11)
Garfield Primary School

THERE IS A CHILD IN MY CLASS

There is a child in my class,
He is always talking and talking,
He has so much to tell.
Even in assembly,
He is constantly getting told off.
And when he has nothing to say,
He'll find something.
At playtime,
When he is playing football,
He is always talking,
That is why he is not so good!
And once he fell asleep,
When the teacher was doing a lesson,
He talked as if he was awake.

Satya Keshani (10)
Garfield Primary School

FLYING

Death, a sad day, the body of a man is lost
The soul lives on stronger than before as it floats up into the sky
Birds swoop by on the breeze not knowing where they will end
The wind carries him up, up to the sunlit sky, up to the heavens
The dreamy blue sky gives him hope as he travels ever upwards
A hot air balloon passes by, children crying out happily,
The journey comes to an end as he reaches the golden gates of heaven
He looks down at the world slowing drifting away.

Peter Richardson (11)
Garfield Primary School

MY FRIEND BLACKY

My friend Blacky is a dog,
He has a cat friend called Mog.
Blacky and Mog play with the frogs in the garden,
Whenever the frogs croak they say pardon.

Blacky's favourite dish is fish,
But he also eats meat.
Blacky has a bird friend called Pete,
But Pete does not eat meat.

Once Blacky offered Pete meat,
But he turned away
And flew to Bombay
As he did not like meat.

Blacky is always friendly and happy,
And whenever he sees me he barks happy
When I come back from school I normally play pool
But when Blacky is awake we play, play, play!
When Blacky wants to stop, he drops.

I love my dog very much
So remember
A pet is for life
And not just for Christmas.

Raam Gulabivala (10)
Garfield Primary School

IMAGINE

Imagine if this world was topsy-turvy,
Where dogs could talk,
Or fish could walk,
Maybe a cat wore a dress,
Now this is a mess.

Imagine if colours were the opposite,
Now this is weird isn't it?
Maybe trees were red,
Yeah, that's what I said,
Or grass pink
What do you think?

Rebecca Ellington (9)
Garfield Primary School

SCHOOL

I like my school
because the teacher's are small.

I like computers because they
are fascinating and interesting.

Some of my friends can be good
and some bad.

The trips that we go on are
brilliant and enjoyable.

I like school.

Ozge Sac (10)
Garfield Primary School

SUMMER

Swimming in the pool,
Gets you cool.
Ice cubes in drinks make it cold.

I feel like I am licking an ice-cream,
I go to the seaside and play with the sand,
I build a sandcastle and I go to the sea and have a swim.
I go back home and invite my friends, play in the garden.

Flowers and plants open and grow
I see in the garden bluebells and other flowers.
I wear shorts and T-shirts
Because it is summertime!

Yeun-Ting Cheung (9)
Garfield Primary School

COUNTRIES

C   ontinents all over the world.
O   ver the world are cold and hot countries.
U   nited States of America is a hot country.
N   ew Zealand feels like paradise.
T   all palm trees in the sandy hot islands.
R   evolting parts of Australia have horrible crocodiles.
I   reland is part of the British Isles.
E   lephants come from Africa and India.
S   audi Arabia is the home of Muslims' God.

Imad Ahmed (10)
Garfield Primary School

SPRINGTIME

The days are getting longer,
The nights are getting shorter,
There is a little more sunshine,
And a little less rain water.

The countryside is looking brighter,
Baby animals are being born,
The daffodils are in full bloom,
Crocuses are appearing on the lawn.

The trees are beginning to grow their buds,
The sunshine makes me smile,
The daffodils go on for more than a mile.

Shelley Ladd (9)
Garfield Primary School

AUTUMN

Autumn is a time for hibernation,
Leaves fall on the ground,
Trees sleep and droop down.
Autumn is a colourful time,
To pick conkers and have some fun,
Look forward to a cold Christmas with my mum.

Winter comes next,
Autumn so colourful and beautiful,
You can't
   not like . . .
      Autumn.

Sophie Jacovou (10)
Garfield Primary School

NATURE

Mother Nature, the mother of all life,
Plants, flowers, trees,
Nature gives new life,
Mammals and others, itchy with fleas.

Sun, the source of all our light,
Nature, sweet and beautiful,
Animals hibernating,
Amphibians and reptiles chasing around the pool.

Flowers blooming in wondrous colours,
Released birds,
Plants of all colours and shapes,
Farmers watching over herds.

Nature.

Jennifer Lane (10)
Garfield Primary School

I SAW A LITTLE PUPPY

I saw a little puppy calling people names.
I saw a stinky rat at a summer wedding.
I saw a clever person screeching her head off.
I saw a big moon calling people names.
I saw a naughty boy who was the thinnest lady
                                in the world.
I saw a fat monkey, chasing a ginger and white cat.

Kunal Shah (8)
Garfield Primary School

I SAW A BABY DOLPHIN

I saw a baby dolphin on my small bedroom floor.
I saw an orange coat shouting at some children.
I saw a green frog flying around in a cave.
I saw a fierce lion mucking around in school.
I saw a grumpy man croaking in a smelly pond.
I saw a brown dog with people working on it.
I saw a grey table walking up and down the busy street.
I saw some skinny girls jumping through a hatch.

Faye Chapman (9)
Garfield Primary School

I SAW A BEAUTIFUL RAINBOW

I saw a beautiful rainbow in Shoe Express.
I saw a shiny shoe with big blue eyes.
I saw a thin boy high up in a dark sky.
I saw a spooky house swimming in a calm deep sea.
I saw a pretty girl shining over a haunted house.
I saw a white cloud sitting in a large field.
I saw green grass flying across an old church.
I saw a sad pig wearing a long dress.

Rita Veghela (9)
Garfield Primary School

TEACHER'S TORMENT

Pay attention, Khurram
Pay attention Sue.
Jay, stop that chattering!
We have things to do.

I can hear a whisper.
Please, all concentrate.
Would you all stop talking children
I am getting a headache.

Armin would you stop being rude
Otherwise you might have to be moved.
Sarah stop chattering with Jay
Or you'll miss your play time for a day.

Today class we will be doing
Words and spellings
But if you don't concentrate this time
I'll send you to Miss Wellings.

Shelly stop chewing your bubble gum,
Or a letter of complaint will go to your mum.
Angelo, Christopher, Sunil, Sophie, stop making that noise
Because you're all acting like noisy toys.

Natter . . . natter . . . natter,
No wonder teachers scold.
As champions of chatter,
You'd win Olympic gold!

Did you know that the high hovering hawk,
Can spy tiny creatures in the grass,
Nearly as quickly as my teacher can spot
People not doing their work in class.

Jay Shetty (10)
Garfield Primary School

ENERGY

Energy is life.
Energy is everything.
Whether it's kinetic or it's nuclear
Or even if it's electric,
But really you shouldn't forget
Light and heat and sound.
Hydropower also exists
That's water power if you didn't know
Use energy wisely or you could end up in trouble.
Energy.

Jonathan Waldheim (10)
Garfield Primary School

SCHOOLS

S   is for schools where you can learn more.
C   is for canteen where you eat your lunch.
H   is for hall where you have assemblies and have PE lessons.
O   is for offering to do something for someone.
O   is for a teacher who is occupied by year six.
L   is for library where you get books to read.
S   is for speaking out even when you are shy in class.

Sunil N Tailor (10)
Garfield Primary School

THE GRENADE

In the autumn of 1915, Friday, 13 November, 17.30 pm

I stood on that hill and watched the shells fly past me.
Half an hour later everything was the same,
So was the next and the next . . .
Then suddenly . . .
Ouch! Something struck me in the stomach
It was a voice coming from the trench below me,
Chanting my name out, over and over again.
This was annoying me so I loaded my rifle with a bullet and I went
into the trench.
I looked all around, but I didn't see a thing.
Then I heard a big *Bang* behind me
I looked up and saw that on the previous spot I was standing on,
Stood a lonely smoke sizzling grenade.

Amir Ali Moussavi (1)
Highgate Junior School

EVENING IN FRANCE

The night is black the moon is bright as the dark clouds pass through it.
When you look up you can see the glistening stars hanging there like
diamonds.
As you walk down towards the beach you can feel the stone-cold air
and hear the crickets chirping.
When you are on the beach you can see the waves crashing against
the shore.
And you can hear the seagulls flap their wings and fly away.

John Edmunds (11)
Highgate Junior School

DO I FIT IN?

Dear diary, why am I dweeby?
I have no friends,
It's not fair,
Tommy has too many friends,
Is it because of my glasses,
Or do I speak differently
I have good English and I am clever,
Oh why is it me?

Should I be good at football?
Or be really naughty,
Maybe I should be horrid like him,
Be rude,
And use bad words,
I will speak now just like him,
This just ain't fair, no it ain't!

Or should I be dumb,
And get minus marks,
Maybe then I will fit in,
Should I do their homework,
Then they will be just like me,
They will just get 'A's,
Hopefully they will be friends with me.

Adam Bitel (10)
Highgate Junior School

SUNRISE - VARANASI GANGES

'Twas all silent in my boat that dawn;
As the golden pearl shone brightly
Upon the soft blue sky.

The silent ripples of the river,
Were suddenly all broken;
By chanting bells
To wake-up the *gods* in the
Himalayan background

People fled to the river
To bathe in it,
And to carry out prayers.
Once again, the silence
had been broken!

Atul CR Dhupelia (11)
Highgate Junior School

EVENING: IN THE BUSH

The sun goes down, the hornbills are at rest,
The zebra's stripes fade into the darkness,
Two glowing eyes appear like bright stars,
Tonight those eyes are on the prowl
Up ahead an impala stops,
Fear in its heart,
The evening's breeze brings danger in its way,
Silently springing,
The leopard confronts the quivering creature,
The moon and stars look down.
They've seen it all before.

Tom James Rodwell (10)
Highgate Junior School

TIME

Why is it I wonder
That time drags so slow
When there is work to do
Nothing exciting, nothing new.

The slow ticking of the clock
Watching its hands hardly move
Waiting for the final release of the bell
Why lessons are so long, I cannot tell

And yet when I play football with my friends,
Sit in the Cinema, watch TV,
It seems the hours and minutes fly
How can this be, I wonder why.

A holiday I wish would never end
Christmas, Easter, my own birthday
Life is strange that all good things
Pass so quickly as if on wings.

And I am left to wonder
If time will stay like this or
In days to come the mystery will unfold
And all days will be the same when I am old.

James Stewart (10)
Highgate Junior School

MY HELL

My hell,
Being surrounded by impatient babies,
Screaming loud and clear,
Nagging for this and that,

In bed hearing echoes of my parents arguing,
Arguing about me or my brother.

Trying to sleep while thinking a burglar is
going to come in and steel everything,
Everything in my house gone.

Going to hospital knowing you're going to have
an operation,
Smelling the hospital, getting nearer.

Waiting to receive your test sheets,
You know this is your weakest subject,
Knowing you're not going to get a good mark.

Getting lost, alone with nobody around you,
Waiting for your parents,
I know what it feels like.

Alberto Fraquelli (11)
Highgate Junior School

THE DARK PARK

Here I am lying in the dark.
Right in the middle of the park.
I watch the birds swooping down.
Looping, hooping through the sky
I wonder how they fly and why?

If I could fly
I would travel the world
Gliding through the everlasting sky.
I'd fly to the moon looking down
At the everlasting darkness.
Thinking where to go next.
Oh why! Why can't I fly.

Luke Solomou (11)
Highgate Junior School

MY HELL

My hell would be lots of snakes, slugs, worms, maggots and
disgusting things like that.
My irritations are people annoying me
Having to pop my ears on a plane
And headaches
My hell is when Chelsea lose
My hell is having stitches or an amputation
My hell is being tortured
Or stabbed
And when I can't do my homework.

Why do we have to go to hell,
I wish I had one more chance
I wish I had done better
And been a lot less evil.

My hell is sharks in the sea and jelly fish and eels
My hell is doing a parachute jump
The parachute not opening
My hell is to stop breathing and suffocate.

William Armstrong (11)
Highgate Junior School

POPPING THE BIG QUESTION

I knew I had to ask now.
The adrenaline pumped through my veins.
What if I dropped it?
What if she said no?
My idyllic reputation could start to diminish.
I went over the wording again and again.
My own saliva cut the air from my throat.
I was soaking wet; what if she noticed the dark clammy marks?
Now I must go to her.
I bent over. Oh my knee!
What next?
Ah yes, get her attention.
I cleared my parched vocals.
Silently she turned to me, like a spider.
I was caught in her web.
I knew then I had to ask.
Softly, tenderly I spoke the words,
'Oi, boss, can I go for me lunch break now?'

Jack Browning (11)
Highgate Junior School

THE GUNFIGHT

My hat kept the sun from my eyes,
The clock struck one;
If I didn't beat these guys,
The town's independence would be none.

Fear filled me from head to toe,
As I reached for my gun;
I tried to pull out but my body said no,
Or the town's independence would be none.

As I shouted the word, 'Draw!'
I was caught in a lassoo;
Then they pulled and I hit the floor,
Knowing the town's independence was going too.

Then they started to jeer and jeer,
Until I lost my gut;
But then the only thing I could hear,
Was, 'That's wrong. *Cut!*'

Oliver Joel Marks (11)
Highgate Junior School

IN THE EVENING

In the evening after dark
All the dogs come out to bark

While we all prepare to sleep
The bats awake and start to creep

The full white moon it shines so bright
And all the owls begin their flight

The gravestones in the churchyard creak
While rats appear and start to squeak

All the goblins look around
Hoping they shall not be found

The homeless huddle in a corner
Wishing they were somewhere warmer

The drunks head home their drinking done
Would they like another one?

Toby Montague (11)
Highgate Junior School

A Suffolk Cottage Evening

As the sun is setting
The fire is burning out;
The owl hoots
And birds sing their song of sleep.

      The wind whistles as it blows through
         the reeds at the side of the pond,
      A frog takes a late night dip;
      And the logs in the shed are wet
         with the evening damp.

The smells of food cooking in the Aga
Wafts through the cottage;
The fresh logs crackle in the grate,
But then silence . . .

Thoe Muller (11)
Highgate Junior School

Evening: Loret De Mar, Spain

As we walk along the esplanade by the sea,
I can hear the crickets chirping in the trees.

Streaks of orange spread out across the sky,
And the sun in the middle like a giant eye.

Seagulls' cries are carried in the air,
It ruffles my trousers, T-shirt and hair.

The sea flows back and is still,
Then it catches a wave like a little moving hill.

The sun is swallowed up without a trace,
It now shines on a different place.

Louis Wallinger (10)
Highgate Junior School

A Day Sailing

The water's smooth,
Our ship is still.
We board our craft,
And wait in hope.
We need a wind,
To fill our sails.
Is that a breeze?
Quick haul that rope!

Cast-off, cast-off,
We must go with this wind,
Or else we'll have to row!
We'll sail along,
With our ship close-hauled,
And set our course,
For the wide open sea.

Our hearts are light,
And full of song.
But what is this?
The sky's turned black
And clouds are forming.
We'd better get back
But here comes the rain.
The first raindrop falls
Right on my nose!

Guy Kirkpatrick (10)
Highgate Junior School

THESE I HAVE LOVED

Soft toys and crayons.
Warm glowing fires with
Yellow and red flickering flames,
Like dancers on a deep black stage.
When everybody's merry on New Year's Day.
The smell of a pizza when you open the box.
The mellow sound of really deep blues.
Cuddling up to watch TV with
My warm, soft, fat, cat.
Bandannas on dogs, they look so cute.
The thrill of gliding over a two-foot jump
On a cantering horse.
Watching *The Simpsons.*
Need I say more
About the things
That I enjoy?

Laurence Powell (11)
Highgate Junior School

EVENING: AT SEA

I was on a boat on a windy night,
We had run out of supplies and could no longer fight,
And there was no other boat anywhere in sight.
The captain said, 'I wish someone would put an end to our
                                                  tragic plight.'

Then things got worse,
A storm evolved,
The captain thought we were under a curse,
It seemed our problem could not be solved.

There were lightning bolts and thunder claps,
The storm continued without a lapse,
My thoughts were of impending doom.
This boat was going to sink very soon.

Why did I ever go to sea?
I wish this boat had never left the quay
Why did I leave, I couldn't have been sane,
I'll never set foot on a boat again.

Nicholas Sowemimo (10)
Highgate Junior School

DON'T THINK I'M A SISSY

There I was, sitting at the back of the class
Red like blood,
What should I do?
Where should I go?
All these questions going on around my head.
Now the teacher is on to the next column,
Getting closer to me.

> I took another look at my book,
> Then at my teacher,
> Then a pool of sweat next to my book.
> Four boys till me,
> I'm still adding to my poem.

Now on to me, the questions came back;
What should I do?
Where should I go?
I went up, shaking.
When I started it I thought why did I think this?
I actually loved it!
I knew I could get through it, well sort of!

Bobby Morris (10)
Highgate Junior School

SOMETHING STRUCK

The weary man had been walking,
For days and nights,
He came across a giant wood,
He heard a scream,
'Who's there?' he shouted.
But all the man heard was a crash,
The man shouted again and yet again,
But still no answer only a growl and a howl,
The weary man walked slowly into the wood,
Something began to move.
'Who's there?' the man shouted.
He looked around but saw nothing,
The man felt a light puff of air on his neck,
He turned round yet again,
But he never knew what struck him.

Jordan Lewis (10)
Highgate Junior School

DRUGS

It comes in all shapes and sizes
And to many it is a killer,
We must resist whatever the temptation
Even though to some it is a thriller.

Some come as tablets, some come as powder
Injections also, whatever the power.
I know I mustn't take it and I must stay clean
Even though all around me there is a dirty scene.

Hospital and prison is where we will end
If we are not careful and tempted by our friends
I don't want to be part of the crowd
If what they do won't make me proud.

I have a life in front of me
And I am surrounded by people who care
I shall make everyone proud of me
And show them there is no need to follow a dare.

Jamie Cohen (11)
Highgate Junior School

A QUESTION UNANSWERED

A dark cloud overlaps the bright
sudden shine of the sun.
The fields darken as sleek hares leap
into their holes.
The Earth stops, as the trembling
rumble occurs.

The mile long stone sitting there
25 metres into the ground.
Parents missing their children playing
with toys.
Rain washed away small rock particles
and there lay an old man's arm.

A fleet of massive trucks pulled
the stone out of the way.
Bodies and flat ranches lay still,
silent in their shadows.
Why them? Why not me? That will be
a question unanswered.

Chase Burns (10)
Highgate Junior School

I WISH

As the car headlights sweep the dusty roads,
And roll over gravel drives.
As the hungry owl swoops to catch a wet, slimy toad,
And picks it up with his powerful claws.
I sit on my chair and stare out the window,
And wish upon a star, that I were a shark swimming in
The deep blue sea.
Where nothing could possibly bother me.

As the clouds swim past the dreamy sun,
And the lights all fade away.
As a fieldmouse runs around having fun,
And dives in and out of hay.
I sit on my chair and stare out the window,
And wish upon a star, that I were a mountain,
As high, as high could be,
Smiling down on everyone, as they all smile up at me.

It's a shame I can't be all those things,
And I know I never will be, but I can always lie in bed at night,
Lie absolutely still,
And wish that I was someone good, to make my heart fulfilled.

Nicholas Voegt (11)
Highgate Junior School

MY LOST LOVE

Her name was Rachel,
She was my lost love.
We'd had really good times together,
But now she's gone
The night before she died,
I had proposed,
She had said yes,
But that's no use now.

Most nights I lie down on the ground,
Thinking about her,
And the time we spent together.
But then remembering,
She will never come back
And I will not be the same without her.

Ladi Lampejo (10)
Highgate Junior School

OCEAN WAVES

The moonlight shimmers down,
Cutting a path through the ocean floor.
The waves roll over each other,
Clambering to get to the shore.
Out of the waves a jet black dolphin jumps up,
And out of the water to end the passing day.
The last boat chugs itself into a lonely dock
To rest after a long hard day's work.
Like a sheet of soft black velvet,
The sea silently engulfs the jagged rocks.
A lighthouse stands out like a ribbon
Clinging onto a lonely stretch of land
In a huge field of waves.
Everything is quiet
Through the whole dark sleeping world
Apart from the sound of the
Softly
Swirling
Ocean
Waves.

Adam Simmonds (11)
Highgate Junior School

DANGER DOWN TOWN

In the far distance a pane of glass shattered
And cabinets of rich jewellery scattered.

Now as the evening draws near
People feel fear.

They assemble and cry,
They may even die.

Inside the raided shop, scattered on the floor
Shining gold, red rubies and more.

Behind a locked door
People lie on the floor.

Arms raised and pleading
The burglar unheeding.

In the dark damp street
Busy people are busy on their feet

Mobile phones singing,
Loud alarms ringing.

A dark and large figure storms out into the street,
Gun pointing, steady and neat.

A motorbike comes near,
The thief dives and makes his get away clear.

Tom McAdam (10)
Highgate Junior School

EXECUTION

One sad and moonlit night
Walking down the corridor
Knowing,
Soon I'll be dead.

I've spent ten years
In this draughty prison
I'm here for something
I didn't do.

I'm here because they said
I killed a cop,
They put me straight on death row
The time's drawing near.

I hear the faint ticking
Of a clock
I think of my wife
My children , my life.

The lights go out
Another one's dead
They lead me in
I see the chair.

I sit down
They strap me in
One last time
For a pra . . .

Simon Malone (10)
Highgate Junior School

SAVED, UNTIL NEXT TIME . . .

The tall dark figure, Rob Jones.
He stands over me with pride,
Sends shivers down my spine.
My legs feel like wobbly jelly,
Everybody backs off.

I urge my friends to help me,
Instead, they just look at me.
The expression on their faces,
Loud and clear. I could read it,
As if they had shouted out loud.
It's my problem.

His shadow blocks the sparkling sun,
And everything turns cold,
I felt like not a bone could move,
I could only watch it pass.

My hair was standing up on end,
And all my skin was goose flesh.
A shout then came from the
Back of the crowd.
I must have heard it wrong,
And yet there it was again.

I could recognise that voice from anywhere,
Miss Painbridge came pushing through.
Jones get off of him,
She urged him towards her study.
I was saved, or should I put it,
Until the next time.

Ben Jacobs (11)
Highgate Junior School

EVENING

Vivid stars glimmer in the night sky
All is still except the glowing moths
Which flutter in the moonlight
A fox scurries through the night
And there is a clatter of a dustbin lid
But again silence as the fox scrambles away.

Once again all is still
Quiet as a soft breeze blowing on the trees
But suddenly from up in the skies
An eerie hoot shatters the silence
A beautiful owl swoops down low
And looks upon the long golden corn.

It glides through meadows
And field mice scurry in all directions
The owl swiftly swoops down
And smoothly picks up a mouse in style
And flies up to the trees
Then not a sound.

Not a whisper from the wind
Not a movement from the birds
All has settled down
All lights are off
The eerie silence is indescribable
Finally evening has settled.

Johnny Dart (10)
Highgate Junior School

EVENING: CARIBBEAN

The sun has gone down, no one's around,
I'm all by myself lying on the ground.
Looking up at the stars in the velvet sky,
I wonder what happens up there so high.
Hearing the waves licking the shore,
What a beautiful night, I think, resting here on the floor.

The sun has gone down, no one's around,
I'm all by myself lying on the ground.
Just the crickets and the grasshoppers are awake with me,
Nothing else at all: a calm company.
Hearing the waves licking the shore,
What a beautiful night, I think, resting here on the floor.

The sun has gone down, no one's around,
I'm all by myself lying on the ground.
Smelling the wonderful sea-salt air
That twists around me like a winding stair.
Hearing the waves licking the shore,
What a beautiful night, I think, resting here on the floor.

The sun has gone down, no one's around,
I'm all by myself lying on the ground.
Wriggling my toes in the soft white sand
And stroking the shells beneath my hand.
Hearing the waves licking the shore,
What a beautiful night, I think, resting here on the floor.

The sun has gone down, no one's around,
I capture the memories, lying here on the ground.

Sam Wild (11)
Highgate Junior School

TEACHERS, WHAT ARE THEY?

Teachers are a different race,
I'm sure they come from outer space.
They have funny smells in their tea,
They always pick on someone, me.
At lunch they eat the strangest cuisines
It's very strange but they seem to like their greens.
They dress in the most unearthly style.
They're the worst fashion icon by a mile.
And have you seen their blackboard pose, it really is a shock,
For if I wasn't used to it I would surely need the doc.
And have you heard them in assembly, it really is a din,
And if I could I'd ban them from committing this wailing sin.
And ten years on I'm used to teachers, yes it's true,
And I can't wait to have children so they can suffer too.

Alexander Taylor (11)
Highgate Junior School

THE CHOCOLATE BOX

Sitting there watching the TV
Suddenly I get a feeling, a craving,
A craving for chocolate
Where does Mum keep it?
Rumbling through the cupboards
Now I remember
I've got my chocolate box
So I go upstairs to my room
The box is full to the brim with chocolate
Scoffing my face with choccies
Dribbling down my throat
Like a river of chocolate
Mmm! Lovely!

Harry Blaiberg (10)
Highgate Junior School

THE HIGHWAYMAN

The wind was howling like a wolf
That dark and rainy night
From nowhere came a stagecoach
Bathed in an eerie light.

Pulled by four phantom horses
They didn't make a sound
They just carried on trotting
As I stood my ground.

I jumped before the stagecoach
And shouted through my fear
'Stop, stand and deliver'
The stagecoach disappeared.

Alex Miller (10)
Highgate Junior School

EVENING: OVER THE SEA

The sea has been playing all day long
Its companions are fishing boats and working men
Children who splash, laugh and shout,
Speedboats, its fast and exciting friends.

Now it is tired and rest must come
The warm night air is its blanket
The breeze, a hand that gently rocks
The sun, its light, is a dim orange glow.

As the sea yawns, it blows leaves on the trees
In its nursery are the silhouettes of daytime toys
Dark old yachts bob in the harbour
Even *young* speedboats are exhausted.

Hamish Edgar (11)
Highgate Junior School

COME BACK TO ME

The last time we said goodbye
Was many days ago
Since that time all I did was cry
And all my feelings were low.

Still our time together went fast
And our time apart has gone slow
I know your feelings for me didn't last
But my feelings for you will not go.

I miss the shine of your golden hair
Your beautiful smile.
And the time that we shared
So I'm writing this note to make sure that you know
That I'm begging for your love
So please, please come back to me.

Luke Vignali (11)
Highgate Junior School

THE LADY OF THE HOUSE

With dead amber in her eyes,
With silence in her heart,
Her skin was as pale as snow,
Her hands as cold as stone.
She glides down the stairs,
And silently around the house,
Into her unknown death.
Over and over again,
Not being able to stop,
Why did it have to be her?

Basil Yannakoudakis (10)
Highgate Junior School

THE EVENING LAKE

Through the mists of a humid summer evening,
Through the towering willow trees.
Past the meadows and beyond.
There lies a lake.

Daytime humming with mosquitoes,
Alive with birdsong.
When dusk falls over the world,
Like a huge blanket,
The lake ceases to hum
Birds quieten.

The slow fading light glints upon the mossy bank.
Buttercups close with a fairy's touch.
The fields of wheat rustle in the evening air.
Bales of hay stand in silent columns.

Dim light dapples through translucent trees,
Falls into the clear waters.
The little fish come out now to play,
Bouncing shells, tittering with the fairies
All is a bustle.

Nightly, when the fish are dreaming
    The moon white and soft
        Falls upon the lake
            He sits there,
                He waits . . .

Tristram Bainbridge (10)
Highgate Junior School

THE NIGHT'S LOTTERY

On a high cliff overlooking the sea,
At night, when I tried to get some rest,
A figure came out, he frightened me,
He came, half hidden, in the mist.

He gave me one wish which I could use,
If I did him a favour,
But I did not know what to choose,
Would he ask something I savour?

I said 'Yes, I'll do that,
But only if you give me a second.'
He shouted 'No, you unreliable rat!'
'He won't give me one,' I reckoned.

But he calmed down and let me think,
I thought of all I would want,
I would like to go for the lottery - and win,
Because if I had the lottery won,

I would build a house in outer space
If I were to win the lottery,
I'd not put it in a piece of pottery,
But use it to get my best dream, space.

But can I use this wish I'm given?
What will this man ask?
'Okay,' I said, to this I was driven
Winning the lottery; for him what a task!

'To win the lottery,' I told him.
'Okay,' he said smiling.
'And now for you to join it,
Go, for me the lottery win!'

Marcus Schofield (11)
Highgate Junior School

THE SEA AT NIGHT

The sea at night is calm, strong and slow,
Waves go on for almost ever.
But when beaches come from far and long,
The sea gets even more annoyed.
Then when the sun comes up,
Everybody throws rubbish in,
The sea wishes they threw it in the bin.
Now the sea wakes up and feels bad,
And then he gets dirty and feels really mad.
The only time the sea can relax
Is in the middle of the quiet, peaceful night.
The only problem without the light,
Is that, straight away, there comes the bright.
So when the morning comes again,
The sea is sad with all the looks.
The sea is now angry
So it splashes and mashes and floods.
Then we all see our mistake
And wish we didn't do it.

Abdulla Mashaal (11)
Highgate Junior School

THE MIDNIGHT HIGHWAYMAN

A horse and rider trot along the path in white moonlight,
Overhanging, grim-faced trees survey the road tonight.
Suddenly the steed bolts upright, paralysed with fright,
But there are no dangers that could frighten him within the rider's sight.

Suddenly, he hears a sound, resounding far away,
A terrible sound, a spectral sound, a ghostly horse's neigh.
With a whinny, and a start, the stallion bolts off in dismay,
And there, along that dark and dusty road, there the rider lay.

And as he lay down on the road, what did the rider see?
A highwayman, in silken clothes, smiling with evil glee.
But when with his evil eyes, no riches did he see,
He mounted up his coal black steed and ran straight over he.

And legend has it that from then on, until this very day,
Along that dark and dusty road, the mangled body lay.

Charles Franklin (11)
Highgate Junior School

IF I HAD THREE WISHES

If I had three wishes,
I would only choose the best for me,
My first wish would be to have a private island,
With a house built over the reef
There would have to be a lagoon not too far out
With one palm tree, the water would be lapping against the golden sand
There would be no clouds in the sky
For that would break the external rays from the sun.

My second wish would have to be
For no more suffering in the world
Because all I want to see is no more war,
And that the homeless and the sad
Would live a life which they never had
There would be no fighting, no stealing and no pain.

My third wish would be to have my soul to live on
Throughout my generations I would be a legend
I would live on through my children's children.
The world would talk about how I had changed it,
For the good of mankind
I gave the homeless and the sick a life
So all I ask for is - to be remembered.

Patrick Rowlands (11)
Highgate Junior School

THE LAST GOLDEN EAGLE

On craggy heights, the eagle's lair,
His cruel, hypnotic, hooded glare,
The proudest, coldest, meanest stare.

Menacing beak, sharp as a spear,
Feathers gleaming, glistening, golden,
In watery sun on a crisp morning clear.

Soaring and sailing, surfing the air,
No mercy, sorrow, love nor care,
Razor talons, that rip and tear.

Groundward he hurtles, past peaks and cliffs,
Glittering light, on sleek black barrels,
Mighty wings beat as the eagle lifts . . .

A gun's deadly blast echoes his shrill cries,
Skims and barrels across blood-red skies,
In watery sun on a crisp morning, he dies.

Joshua Bicknell (10)
Highgate Junior School

EVENING IN A SWISS CHALET

Outside, the soft swirling snow settles silently,
The sun's golden glow makes a halo behind
                            the dark mountains.
The evening is bitter cold and shows no mercy.
Scavenging owls and foxes are out hunting while
                            their young wait impatiently,
Down in the valley lights twinkle,
The searching headlamps of cars are like fireflies.

Inside, everyone is settled,
The warm fire lights up the room and casts
                              flickering shadows.
Books are being read while cats and dogs snuggle
                              next to friendly feet.
Supper is on the way, there are hungry stomachs to fill,
Enticing smells waft from the kitchen.

Alexander Manby (10)
Highgate Junior School

EVENING

Black bats are fluttering past
making no sound at all,
The sun is setting
dropping down behind the hills.
The smell of cherry blossom fades
with the light.
The white cat says 'Au revoir'
and saunters off home.
Shadows of cows against the
fence move to the barn,
a dog barks far away.
Cooler now, wood smoke
steak and frites.
Light darker, dark, the country
is quiet now.

Stewart Allan (10)
Highgate Junior School

FULFILLED?

Last minute goal at Wembley,
Back to school assembly,
Into my Caribbean home
Or I'm in London facing hundreds of problems alone!

I see the ball curl into Arsenal's net,
The pass from Flitcroft was superb,
I saw the ball go past Sam Park's fingertips,
Then in all my fame and glory,
My girlfriend comes and gives me a kiss on the lips.

'Hurry, hurry, you're late for assembly,'
'Don't walk on the grass,
You'll get your feet dirty!'
'Walk in a straight line,
Stop talking!'
'Don't, don't, don't!'

The palm trees sway in the light Caribbean wind,
The sea all crystal blue,
I get a cold drink indoors and then go into a snooze.

'Done this late, that's not on time,'
My mum and dad give support,
But I still feel I need some more!

I go both ways but I find the way I am
To others affects the way they are to me,
Generosity to all other creatures,
And the world will be happy!

Adam Klug (10)
Highgate Junior School

ME

I stare outside my window and,
Wonder why and when?
Why do I feel I am an old man,
Trapped in a child
And how many thoughts come
Into my mind?

How many years will I be
On earth?
Will my soul go to heaven?
Or maybe not.
Which way is my destiny going?
Am I lost for eternity?

Why does nobody take notice of me
In the playground?
Now I feel my nerves of steel
Crumble apart.
Where must I go to find
A good laugh?

Why do I feel my body
Tossed into a sea of nothingness?
Scenes of vast shipwrecks of my senses.
Why can't I get involved?
When will the time come
When I become someone?

Dheeraj Harjani (10)
Highgate Junior School

EVENING: NEW YORK AT CHRISTMAS

New York's night is beginning.
With every new flake of clear white snow
The streets are becoming more crowded
The hustle, bustle is starting.
I walk down 5th Avenue and look into the shop windows
Dazzling jewellery and make-up are stacked on shelves
The Chrysler building dominates the skyline.

Shoppers come out of every store with bags
Niketown, Bloomingdales, Macy's,
Everywhere you look there is something or somebody to interest you,
No one is gloomy at Christmas.

I cross the street, the road is packed with cars and trucks,
Christmas lights are drawing me towards them.
I take a shortcut through Central Park,
Thick snow covers the grass like a blanket
The moon is shining in the starlit sky
All is peaceful now,
I hear the distant rumble of traffic in the background.

Rockefeller Center is suddenly before me
The huge Christmas tree comes into sight
Dizzy, dancing and bright.
I push my way through the crowd to look at the ice rink,
The skaters seem to glide.
I watch and then turn for home.

Alex Dodds (11)
Highgate Junior School

EVENING: SEAHOUSES ENGLAND

The harbour lights illuminate the quay
The air is calm, the gulls no longer cry
The fishing boats are resting from the sea
Their work is done until the next tide is high.

But suddenly a klaxon blasts the air
The lifeboat trundles from its shed
The harbour-master's seen a flare
The lifeboat crew come running from their beds.

An hour or so goes by, the lifeboat is home again
Its powerful engines churning up the sea
A false alarm, they found no remains
Some ship far out quite probably.

Bamburgh lights are turning off
The castle lights stand bright in the night
The waves crash against the rocks hard and soft
The Farne light flashes bright.

The fading sky turns brightness into night
The blue and gold horizon drifts away
The crabs all scuttle out of sight
The whole world rests until the day.

Robert Anderson (10)
Highgate Junior School

MOUNT ETNA ERUPTS

I woke up hearing rumbles and crumbles
For the trouble had just begun,
For Mount Etna had awoke with anger and madness,
For smoke and ash came out of his head.
Mother never woke up,
Mother was in a deep sleep,
Far from the noise, and far from the adventure.
Then suddenly a blast of lava came out,
For the snake slid down the mountainside.

Mother would always have nightmares of Etna,
With lava pouring into the house,
For the nightmare had come alive.
I was shrugging her, pushing her and lots, lots more.
But she wouldn't wake up.
She had given up on me.

As I saw the lava come down,
Demolishing the museums at the top of the mountain,
I gave up, I left the house,
And left my mother and said 'Goodbye.'
I saw my mother crumble and rumble
As I ran and left her alone.

And now, three years later, I look at the stones of lava,
And somewhere there, her body lies,
Sleeping and left alone.

James Ridgway (11)
Highgate Junior School

WHY?

Why do stars shine bright at night?
Why do people always fight?
Why can't crisps come in two big packs?
Why do old men break their backs?

Why do cats have dirty paws?
Why do young men break the law?
Why are women scared of spiders?
Why not big fat horseback riders?

Why do Greeks wear only sandals?
Why do we use dinner candles?
Why don't we have dirty kings?
Why does wind blow strong in spring?

Nicholas Baker (11)
Highgate Junior School

THE ANTS' NEST

Down, under it's dank and dark,
a rumbling noise wakes ants with a start.
A predator, or could it be the moving roots of a sycamore tree.
Ants that lack the speed they need, never will last long with us,
because ants are brave and ants are tough.

Out on top in the cool fresh air,
just to see who might go there.
There are no roots, there are no trees,
it's a predator on the morning breeze.
Ants that chicken-out above, never will last long with us,
because ants are brave and ants are tough.

Celia Turnbull (11)
Muswell Hill Junior School

SOMETIMES I WONDER

Sometimes I wonder why we're alive, why are we here?
Why are we here in this world?

Sometimes I wonder what my friends are doing?
Why they are alive, why they are here?

Sometimes I wonder why people do such terrible things?
Why they are alive, why they are here?

Sometimes I wonder if fish have thoughts?
Why they are alive, why they are here?

Sometimes I wonder what my cat is thinking?
Why she is alive, why she is here?

Emma Bergamin-Davys (10)
Muswell Hill Junior School

WIND

The wind is an unemotional cheetah,
Cold and unfriendly against the glowing lion of the sun.
Mercilessly dashing faster than a bullet,
Cruelly scattering a flock of birds.

Everyone says that he is a vulgar imp,
But in real life he is just a gloomy cheetah.
Despised and condemned:
He dolefully weeps.

Harry Collins (10)
Muswell Hill Junior School

THE SEASONS

Spring is the green bud of the flower,
Growing among its friends.
Watching over the young animals,
As they happily play around it.

Summer is the flower as it bursts into colour.
The field where it grows is a carpet of bright plants.
They sway in the gentle breeze.
Birds fly over them watching with piercing eyes.

Autumn is the flower as it slowly turns brown,
Watching as other plants do the same.
The fun is over, the sadness begins,
The flowers' time is almost out.

Winter is the brown flower growing weaker.
Snow falls, ice gathers.
Animals are hibernating.
The flower bends and drops to the ground.
There is no life in the field where he lived.
The flower leaves his decaying body,
As a gravestone where he once lived.

Jack Severs (10)
Muswell Hill Junior School

HAPPY DAYS

What makes me happy is when I play sticky toffee with my best friends.
What else makes me happy is when I have chocolate and sweets.
My favourite TV programme always makes me happy.
My teacher makes me smile.

Sarah Varney (8)
Muswell Hill Junior School

AS ICARUS FELL

The farmer sat back in his chair,
He looked around, nothing there.

Icarus fell, like ripe fruit from a tree.
As the seasons passed, so did he.

His body grew rotten, his body grew old,
The fishes ate his flesh, so his body grew cold.

The farmer grew older, but never has he heard,
The story of Icarus, trying to be a bird.

The farmer had a son, and then he died,
Neither he nor his son, heard how Icarus tried.

And so that's the end of this tragic story,
How Icarus flew, yet died in glory.

Dominic Lintner (11)
Muswell Hill Junior School

SHADOW, THE PRINCE OF THE NIGHT

A demon-like figure gliding through the mist,
A black-cloaked rider galloping through the night,
A black mist floating in the sky,
A dark giant eagle flying across the cloud banks,
A silent silhouette rushing in the wind,
A ghostly man sliding across the stars,
A slippery black serpent gliding in the night sky,
A dark shape creeping over the treetops,
A black hole swallowing up the light,
Shadow, the prince of the night.

George Crosthwait (10)
Muswell Hill Junior School

LIGHT AND DARK

A shaft of sunlight peeks in my room,
casts shadows on my bedroom wall
A little bird's tweet tells me it's daybreak
Oh no - it's morning and time to get up soon

I lay in bed a little bit more
Mum comes and knocks on my bedroom door
Time to get out of my warm bed and pop on some clothes
Jumper, leggings and socks on my toes

Down for breakfast, zooming down banisters,
booming down the stairs, eating quickly and brushing my hair.
Coat on, rush a little bit more, line up at the school door in a nice
group of four.
Doing work, time for lunch, out to play, end of day

Time to go home, it's now getting dark,
The moon's in the sky, no dogs in the park

Late home again, who cares?
All I want to do is be back in bed with my bears.

Esme Newdick (10)
Muswell Hill Junior School

WHAT MAKES ME HAPPY

I like playing on the N64 for hours on end.
My birthday makes me happy.
My brother makes me laugh.
My friends and family make me happy.
My orange hair makes me happy.

Michael Simpson (7)
Muswell Hill Junior School

MRS SPARROW

Mrs Sparrow in the air
Flying around without a care,

Flying, swooping through the sky
Where no one can go, neither you nor I

Breathing in the fresh, cool air
Bumping into air balloons, it's just not fair

Soaring, swooping through a cloud
She has a right to be very proud

As she returns to her child
Still blind but very wild

Sparrows fly very high
So think before you try to fly.

Charlotte Trevor (11)
Muswell Hill Junior School

WHAT MAKES ME HAPPY

Enjoying things like bike-riding makes me jolly.
Christmas makes me feel great.
Craft work makes me feel lovely.
Isabelle and Rachel make me feel great.
TV makes me very jolly.
Ice-creams make me feel great.
Noises makes me happy
Gifts make me feel great.

Eleanor Morgan (8)
Muswell Hill Junior School

OPEN THE DOOR

Open the door
Maybe you'll see
Mum baking a cake just for me
With a golden-brown crispy top.
Or maybe you'll see
an ugly old goblin drinking some tea.
But don't be afraid.
go and open the door.
Open the door
Maybe you'll see
Dad reading the paper
His head buried in the pages.
Or maybe you'll see
an octopus watching TV,
with eight drinks,
one in each hand.
But don't be afraid
Go and open the door.

Mathilda Holt (7)
Muswell Hill Junior School

MY HAPPY POEM

Playing on Sega Saturn makes me happy
My friends make me happy
Rollerblading makes me happy
My family makes me happy
Watching TV makes me happy
I like playing 'It' with my best friends
I like Sarah because she makes me laugh
That makes me happy.

Elaina Ioannou (8)
Muswell Hill Junior School

COLOURS

Blue is winter,
Cold and wet.
I'm watching from the window,
As the slushy ice sets.

Green is spring,
Full of life.
See the trees reach up,
Into the wispy skies.

Yellow is summer,
Full of heat.
Filling music with a friendly beat,
And friendly people you will meet.

Red is autumn,
Windy and crisp.
Trees are dropping all their leaves,
So we wrap up or we'll begin to sneeze.

Charlotte Whittlestone (11)
Muswell Hill Junior School

MAKES ME HAPPY

When I see my little hamster looking out the bars of the cage
I think of playing with the little bundle of fun.
She runs to the end of my bed, she would not dare to jump off.
She would just run back into my hand.
Handling her makes me happy, then I put her in the cage.
I like her running on the wheel.
I like to watch TV and bumble bees.
I like to see the trees blowing in the breeze.

Camille Freemantle (7)
Muswell Hill Junior School

THE SEASONS

Spring is a baby,
Changing all the time,
Some days it cries,
Some days it's full of joy,

Summer is a bumble bee,
Happily buzzing around,
It's always busy,
It greets all the flowers with a happy smile
as it gives them lots of pollen,

Autumn is a rusty, red apple,
Its peel flaking off to the ground,
The peel is red, gold and brown,
It crunches as it falls to the ground,
And the apple slowly gets smaller and colder,

Winter is a hungry wolf, eating all the sunlight,
It shadows the world with an angry stare,
As it covers the sun it gets colder and colder,
Leaving the world to freeze.

Anna Mayer (11)
Muswell Hill Junior School

WHAT MAKES ME HAPPY

Football makes me happy.
Games also make me happy too.
Computer games make me happy
And also eating eggs.
Being good and watching Robin Hood
makes me happy too.

Alexander Kay (8)
Muswell Hill Junior School

NIGHT AND DAY

The sun is a golden mare, rearing up at the thought of encagement.
Honey-coloured, neighing softly, she awakens and spreads her glory.
Midday arrives, and her fury shows, her mane flaring and casting
                                                    heat over the world.
In the evening, she calms down and scrapes away the blue field
to show the black soil, studded with white roots.
She gallops away and her brother, the black stallion of night,
arrives in his kingdom. A day has passed.
When the golden mare gallops behind the hills, the black stallion
                                                    awakes.

He draws his might all over the mare's blue fields
and eats the white roots left for him by his sister.
He is wild, untamed, but in the morn,
the mare returns once more.
A night has passed.

Lottie Young (10)
Muswell Hill Junior School

WHAT MAKES ME HAPPY

My friends make me happy.
When I watch TV I am happy.
When I look in my pond at the waterfall
and fountain, it makes me happy.
I like to look at patterns because it makes me smile.
I really like riding my bike.
I really like it when I have my best food.

Sophie Gainsley (8)
Muswell Hill Junior School

OPEN THE DOOR

Open the door,
Perhaps you'll see . . .
your mum taking your dog
for a walk.
Or maybe you'll see . . .
a vampire staring back at you.
Open the door, perhaps you'll see . . .
a dog chasing a cat,
or maybe you'll see . . .
a ghost with blood on its teeth.
But don't be afraid
go and open the door.

Alexandra Lambis (7)
Muswell Hill Junior School

WHAT MAKES ME HAPPY

Playing on my PC for hours and hours makes me happy.
Watching TV makes me very happy.
Rollerblading is fun.
When I go outside on my bike I get really happy.
When I spend my money I am very happy.
Playing outside makes me happy.
Reading makes me very happy.
I like going to Grimsby.
Drawing makes me happy.

Ashley Scillite (7)
Muswell Hill Junior School

THE BEAR

Morning comes, the bear awakes,
Kills the salmon and eats its steaks.
Running after his mid-morning snack,
He swipes, he misses and falls on his back.
It's getting hot, he goes in the river,
The water is cold and he starts to shiver.
Dusk is breaking, it's getting dark,
He sees some honey engraved in the bark.
He leaps, he clings and climbs to the top,
He gets some honey and falls with a plop.
Now he finds it's bees he hears,
They fly after him and sting his ears.
So at the end of the day he's feeling sore,
He feels his day has been rather poor.

Marcus Newdick (11)
Muswell Hill Junior School

THE SEA

I perceive the sea with its beckoning cries,
I marvel at its deep depths,
I have jealousy because of its secrets,
The sea has inconsiderate waves,
they tumble down like a herd of unicorns
The sea is indigo
Beneath its depths, are the debris of ships,
destroyed, ruined and shattered to bits.

Cira Gaber (11)
Muswell Hill Junior School

An Old Man

An old man walks down the street,
Greeting all the people that he meets.
He walks down the old country lane.
Memories of his family flood back to him again.

He staggers and falls onto a bench,
His walking-stick he still has to clench.
He falls asleep in a daze.
Thinking of all the children he helped to raise.
A woman sits down and wakes him up,
He thanks her again and again, and then starts off
down the country lane.

Lindsey Mendick (10)
Muswell Hill Junior School

The Train

The bang and clatter,
the hum and patter,
the babies crying,
the mothers sighing,
the people walking,
the people talking,
we're at the station now,
everything's *stopped.*

Joanna Matheson (10)
Muswell Hill Junior School

LIGHT AND DARK

Devils stalking through the fire all red and hot.
Evil fills the misty, dark midnight air.
Violent fire, burning everything in sight.
In the evil eye of a devil all you can see is ebony death.
Light fills the sky, as the devils cry in agony.

Ancient angels flutter around.
Neat feathery bright landings.
Gentle beams of light following near and far.
Elegant haloes shining proud.
Light disappears, for it's time for the devils again.

Amna Siddiqui (9)
Muswell Hill Junior School

THE SUN

The sun is a chick that gives
birth to each day
Its yellow fur is like burning-hot fire
It walks across the sky as each day goes past.

As it pecks at the clouds,
it grows rounder and bigger each day.

As the day slowly ends the chick goes to sleep,
The light turns into dark, the sun turns into the moon,
ready for a new day to begin.

Simone Woolerton (11)
Muswell Hill Junior School

OPEN THE DOOR!

Open the door and maybe you'll see
Cars zooming down the road
Glistening in the sunlight, polluting the air
Or maybe you'll see a roast chicken dinner just waiting for me.

Open the door and maybe you'll see
A naughty child who wants to watch TV
But we could open the door to fantasy land
And visit a palace that looks very grand.

Open the door and maybe you'll see
A mouse scuttling up to me.
Or maybe you'll see
An ugly old witch (who lives in a ditch)
Making herself a cup of frog and bat tea.

Open the door and maybe you'll see
Some trees swaying in the wind.
Or maybe you'll see
A herd of charging buffalo.

But don't be afraid don't shake with fear
Just open the door.

Alice Engelhard (7)
Muswell Hill Junior School

A CLOUD

A cloud is a massive ball of cotton wool soft and fluffy.
It is a sheep, walking across the sky, peacefully being softly
pushed across the sky never going to fall.
A cloud is a splash of white ink on blue card.
A cloud is God's mattress.

Niall O'Neill (11)
Muswell Hill Junior School

OPEN THE DOOR

Open the door perhaps you'll see
a fire-breathing dragon watching TV.
Open the door you might see a classroom
full of children working so quietly you
can't hear a sound.
Open the door you might see a witch
on a broomstick as black as night
with her out-stretched cloak.
Open the door and you might see
mummies pushing prams in a nursery.
Open the door and you might see a
giant doing exercises with a plaster
on his knee.
Open the door and you might see a
nanny knitting a scarf for a little girl
who is very cold and has no home.
She is very sad.
Open the door and you might see aliens
having a disco and screeching so loud.
Open the door and you will see the poem
that I've written just for you.

Sophie Volhard (7)
Muswell Hill Junior School

TORNADO

A tornado is like a snake slashing around eating anything in its way.
It's like an anaconda swerving around destroying anything possible.
Wind like a snake shaking its tail.
Spraying poison on houses destroying everything.
Spinning round, stunning everyone, lifting and swerving.

Alexi Emery (11)
Muswell Hill Junior School

INSIDE ME . . .

Inside me there is a bull charging at my friends,
And a quiz, tickling my thoughts,
Inside me there is a dove filling my heart with love and hate,
And a lion speaking careless words,
Inside me is an eagle protecting all my feelings,
And a rainbow lighting up my face,
Inside me is a waterfall of tears kept behind my eyelids,
And a tree growing every day,
Inside me is a mouse which is sometimes shy,
And a monkey doing naughty tricks,
Inside me is a fire burning in the pit of my stomach,
And a page turning each new day.

Megan Cowles (10)
Muswell Hill Junior School

OPEN THE DOOR

Open the door and see
What is there.
It's a white ghost who stares at me at night
or is it my mum who has put off the light?
Just open the door and see what is there,
Is it a tiger who's growling at me?
Or is it a wolf howling its head off?
Just open the door. It is a pig doing a jig.
Or is it a man eating a fig?
Just don't be afraid. Just open the door.

Ffion Knaggs (8)
Muswell Hill Junior School

OPEN THE DOOR

Open the door.
Perhaps you'll see.
A postman.
Or even a witch on her broomstick.
Or maybe a cat jumping through the window.
Or even some aliens who come from the planet Jupiter,
who plan to take over the earth.
Or a milkman quietly putting it on the doorstep.
And the cat coming out fiercely to get the milk.
Don't be afraid just open the door.

Leslie Manu (8)
Muswell Hill Junior School

THE BUBBLE

Bobbing up and down like a fisherman's float,
Blowing slower than the slowest boat.
A see-through air balloon with no basket to pull it down,
Pink, blue, green and brown.
Resting in the air on a carpet of nothing,
Bending bubbly ears to hear the birds sing.
Smoothly floating silently.
Up ahead a tree!
The little bubble cannot stop,
Drifting closer then suddenly . . . *Pop!*

Natasha Rosenbaum (11)
Muswell Hill Junior School

POEM

The poem is a colossal, terrifying lion
I try to avoid,
But with a magnificent leap,
It springs from a bush.

The words are fleas,
Hopping around its mane
The rhymes are powerful legs,
Pounding after prey
The rhythm is its teeth,
Gnawing at a bone.

I put down the poem,
And the lion leaves
With a roar of satisfaction.

Adam Guy (10)
Muswell Hill Junior School

OPEN THE DOOR

Open the door and perhaps you'll see.
An ugly wart-nosed witch with green eyes
and a black face.
Or perhaps you'll see elves joining hands,
spinning in a circle.
But don't be afraid
go and open the door.
Open the door and perhaps you'll see
a ghost driving a car.
Wooooooooooooooooh.

Lauren Brighton (8)
Muswell Hill Junior School

THE ROARING WIND

The wind is a lion
roaring through
the sky
eating at the trees
as he goes
by
pounding his paws
as he
roars
brushing the clouds
with his hairy
mane
and the roaring
wind still
remains.

Nicola Shields (10)
Muswell Hill Junior School

OPEN THE DOOR

Open the door
Perhaps you'll see lemmings jumping.
Trees dancing in the wind.
And the rain outside falling down.
You might see the wild witch of the west,
with her hair all black and knotted.
Maybe you'll see a fire-breathing dragon.
But don't be afraid.
Maybe you'll see the sun shining
its very brightest.

Georgina Gainsley (8)
Muswell Hill Junior School

THE SUN

The sun is a golden lion, stalking the moon.
In the morning it abandons its lair and peeps over the hill,
The moon sees the great, red, fiery mane, rushing along the hill,
The moon is the cheetah of the sky, leaving as quickly as it comes,
It bounds through the night and into the safety of its tree,
The sun pounces after the moon but finds itself stuck in the sky.
It roars and sends out a fiery light which ignites the world below,
Moles and shrews scramble into their homes, afraid of the sun,
The humans wake and start their pointless chores.
The sun is enraged and his anger flows down on the world in the
form of heat.
And then the sun falls into its kingdom,
The moon is coming back but the sun is too tired to chase it,
Instead he sits on his haunches and roars his powerful roar,
He returns to his lair, untriumphant again,
He slumps to the floor and his light dims to a soft red, and then
he sleeps.
The moon comes out from the safety of his tree and turns the day
to night,
He is victorious again, but one day, the sun will catch him.

Daniel Graham (11)
Muswell Hill Junior School

SWALLOW

I'm flying through the air
without a care in the world.
Gliding effortlessly, soaring high.
See the people on the ground as small as ants.
Bobbing up and down like an apple on water.
Drifting along with my tail blowing out behind me.

Alexander Stone (10)
Muswell Hill Junior School

DEATH

A dark cloaked figure,
With a scythe at his side,
An overseas stranger,
With a face of pure white,
Eyes that pop out,
With dark-rimmed edges.
When you die, he's by your side,
As much of a stranger as before.
The last few days of your life
are spent thinking of the
overseas stranger,
Until the day you die.
When you lay down your head,
And breathe your last breath,
Then you see the dark cloaked figure,
He leans over you and says
          'I'm death.'

Annie Henderson (10)
Muswell Hill Junior School

SNOW

Snow is icing down on the ground,
Trees are the green icing in little tiny dots,
House tops are cola laces cut up into squares,
When the snow melts, icy grass pokes up like sugar strands,
If you are in a plane, you will see the delicious cake,
But down below then you'll know that all it is, is snow,
Tread in the icing, thick and sweet, up to your knees it goes,
Slide down it on a sledge to write happy birthday.

Laura Simpson (10)
Muswell Hill Junior School

THE STORM

A secluded dog is the storm itself,
Its drool and spit the rain,
The dog growling at the birds
struggling through the storm,
To make the thunder roar,
When the dead hear that sound
they whimper and moan.
Lightning is the dog's yellow glaring eyes,
Clashing against the deep dark sky.
Slowly the storm gets softer,
The tired dog drops on the floor,
For his summer hibernation.
A soft white kitten crawls by his side
and pushes him into his den.
She changes the world to summer,
And looks after it till winter.

Georgina Ward (10)
Muswell Hill Junior School

WINTER

Winter is a cold, dark hand that strangles shrubs and smothers trees.
Winter's fingernails are icicles like frozen swords and icy daggers.
They hang from trees like bats in a dark cave.
Winter's snow is a deadly blanket covering everything, everywhere.
Flowers and plants are swallowed up and drowned.
Suddenly the warm, green spears of spring shoot up through the
blanketing whiteness.
Melting away the cold death and winter's evil reign is no more.

Reuben Dangoor (10)
Muswell Hill Junior School

SWALLOW

I'm a swallow drifting through the air,
flapping my wings through the cold winter air.

I can feel snow falling on my wings,
I am gentle,
I am free.

My feathers all black and white,
They glow when I sweep through the dark,
chilly night.

I soar through the air looking down,
I see all the people who look like little insects
crawling there on the ground.

Camilla Seckin (10)
Muswell Hill Junior School

WHITE DUCK

The smooth cutting of the clouds
Soaring, gliding on a blanket of nothing

Full of white feathers, fluff falls off
slowly into the cool, slow water

The bird of fun, the bird of charm,
Charms you with a flash of its white, white feathers,
The *duck!*
The bird of the quiet farmyard.

Jack Bevington (10)
Muswell Hill Junior School

MY ROAD

The sun twinkling on the metal barrier.
The tall houses towering above me.
Trees that are excellent for climbing.
The tapping on the pavement from passers-by.
The banging front doors.
The freshness of my road because there are no fumes.

The bumpy pavements with all the cracks.
The brown leaves, a memory of autumn still on the road.
The blossom on the trees in spring.
The naked figures of the trees in winter.
The road where I live and always have.

Madeleine Power (9)
Muswell Hill Junior School

SUMMER

Summer is the sun,
a burning marble glowing
all day long.

Summer is a hot, sunny day,
People playing, people sweating.

Summer is for flowers,
blowing, swaying
in the hot air.

Summer is the season
for joy and happiness.

Judy Tumber (10)
Muswell Hill Junior School

THE DRESSING GOWN IN THE NIGHT

The dressing gown behind the door,
Is a big, scary monster about to roar,
Its long, thin tongue is swaying around,
It's floating about with its feet off the ground.
It opens its mouth to welcome me in,
Oh, the scary eyes and the big, mean grin.
At any moment it's going to leap,
And land on my bed in an ugly, great heap.
Then it will eat me up and say,
'If only I could eat him every day.'

Freddy de Lord (10)
Muswell Hill Junior School

THE DOG

The sky is a howling dog with white spots.
Running after the bright yellow ball.
As it gets higher he jumps and catches it in his dark mouth.
As it darkens his white spots light up.
With one eye open and the other closed, he sleeps.
At dusk he opens the other eye and spots another ball.

In winter the dog's coat changes colour from blue to black.
He catches his bright-yellow ball soon after he awakes.
He cries because there is not a thing to do, he cannot wait till spring.

Harriet Phillips (10)
Muswell Hill Junior School

THE WIND

The wind is blowing down my chimney,
It's banging and clattering against the walls.
The wind is rattling through the window,
And it's bitterly waiting until something falls.

The wind is strongly pushing over trees,
It's whistling and tapping,
It's howling at my knees.

The wind is gushing at the washing line,
It's cracking and smacking,
At that jumper of mine.
The wind is so rough.

Harry Wilson (8)
Muswell Hill Junior School

THE SUN

When the other planets see his mane of flames,
They know he will not be fun and games,
From his drooling mouth comes his loud fiery roars,
He hangs in the big, black universe only by his sharp claws,
With his rough, orange coat and his long, fluffy tail,
He definitely is the leading male, the ruler of the universe,
The ferocious king of all, if anyone dare mess with him,
All that will be heard is their very mournful bawl.

Sophie Bond (11)
Muswell Hill Junior School

WINDY WIND

Windy wind lives in the bin
It clatters it shatters
It howls it growls
It gets through gaps
It gets through catflaps
It whistles down chimneys
It whistles through halls
Sometimes it even makes me fall
It's fierce
Very weird
I hate windy wind.

Bruno Downey (9)
Muswell Hill Junior School

NIGHT AND DAY

Night is a pitch-black horse
Galloping through the sky.
Spreading darkness throughout its course
Screaming nightmare in its eye.

Day is a dancing white stallion
Pirouetting in the light.
Streaming like a galleon
In full sail and in all its might.

Abigail Guest (10)
Muswell Hill Junior School

THE FALL OF ICARUS

It was a warm, spring day in Crete,
Icarus was bored.
Fly Icarus, fly, insisted Daedalus,
Don't go too high, the father warned.
Icarus flew and was as happy as ever,
Gliding, soaring, hovering over the clouds,
But then Deadalus's heart filled with bitterness,
Icarus flew and was then plummeted to the ground,
The wax on the wings melting away,
Icarus had flown too high into the hot sun,
The poor boy splashed into the sea,
As his helpless father watched in distress,
Daedalus buried Icarus into the wet, cold ground.

William Thacker (11)
Muswell Hill Junior School

THE SUN

The sun is a ferocious lion glowing in the sky with fiery.
As he savages the crescent moon with his piercing claw.
He looks over the world with wrath and jealousy
As he sees the people jubilant, joyful and free.
But he is imprisoned up in the highest of the sky
for all that he had done to be selfish.
He suddenly starts to be fatigued and slowly starts
to descend.

Anastasia Smith (11)
Muswell Hill Junior School

RAIN

Splish, splash, rain a tongue,
dribbling of thirst,
Scribbling all over the earth,
Digging like a mole,
doing the elephant water roll.
Hitting you like tiny whips,
sometimes even like little lips.
Slash, clash, getting heavier and heavier.
Dying down, lying on the ground.
Massive puddles,
turn into cuddles.

Sam Miles (10)
Muswell Hill Junior School

SPRING

Spring is a fragile fairy,
It flies away so lightly.
There's always a delicate smile
In the baby-blue sky.
The clouds are her wings.
The flowers are her arms.
The green trees are her legs.
The grass is her tummy.
She smells fresh and new.
She sounds calm and peaceful
Especially with the birds whistling and gossiping.

Amy Morris (11)
Muswell Hill Junior School

MY PETS

My new dog Tilly does her own little tricks.
She goes upside down and round.
My other dog Champ wouldn't hurt a fly,
Because he's my little pie.
Now Daisy on the other hand, sits in the corner and cries.
I wonder why? Maybe she's missing her mum,
Or maybe she's all mine.
Becky, she's a lively one,
She barks and moans all day long.
My three cats, Jerry, Harvey and Davison,
Jerry, the mum, they're all black and white.
My two parrots edge towards me as I walk in.
With my two rabbits and my giant fish,
My pets are complete.

Nicola Liddon (11)
Muswell Hill Junior School

THE MOON

A misty silver, a wintry colour is the moon.
The windy wind is milk drifting over someone's lips.
A silver twinkle in the sky reflects off every single fly.
The trickle they call the moon is surrounded by little starry fumes.
It is time to go to bed but the moon stays up instead and looks after the
people who are in their beds.
The sun rises
The moon sets
It's time for the moon to go to bed.

Stephanie Sklavounos (10)
Muswell Hill Junior School

THE NIGHT

The night is a beautiful sleek black cat,
Spreading his colour as he stealthily creeps over the rooftops.
Turning the daylight into darkness as he walks past.
His fur is all shades of black,
His eyes are two shining bright stars.
His paws are enormous and playful,
His pawpads are black soft velvet.
He is dormant in the day,
But comes attentive and alive to hunt at night.
This beautiful creature knows he must suddenly retreat,
For daylight is creeping up behind him.

Olivia Brinson (11)
Muswell Hill Junior School

THE SUN

The sun is a roaring lion,
a fiery temper.
The lion's mane is glowing,
locked up in a burning cage of fire.
His eyes are burning balls of fire.
Jaws of steel, teeth like golden flames.
The door unlocked,
the lion is free,
prowling back to his concealed den
of glowing golden yellow flames.

Kate Sharkey (10)
Muswell Hill Junior School

THE HORSE

Black as night,
like a thunder roll,
The name is Black Beauty.
Charming, fine, elegant, dainty,
galloping through the rushing wind
whistling through her ears.
Her mane flopping in the wind,
shining like polished shoes.
Her elegant figure as black as night,
that's why they call her Black Beauty.

Imogen Fullbrook (11)
Muswell Hill Junior School

ICARUS FALLS

The sun, blazing like a hot cross bun.
Icarus flying fast,
Then he remembered about the past.
'Don't go high or you might just die,'
His dad had told when it was cold.
Now very hot, he felt like a dot.
Icarus was falling as his dad was calling.
When he splashed, his wings crashed.
Now he's dead,
Not if he listened to what his dad said.

Alexander Flower (11)
Muswell Hill Junior School

THE WIND

The wind is a giant,
Rushing through the trees,
Growling and roaring through the woods,
Blowing leaves off a branch.
The wind could be a hurricane,
So strong it makes the waves grow high.
People keep warm as the wind slows down,
This is the giant having a quiet, sweet sleep.
There is still a small wind from the giant's snore.
People are relieved as they swiftly walk back to their homes.
As the giant awakes, he yawns loudly, to bring an after-shock.
People get frightened as he howls through the dark night.

Paula Gloger (10)
Muswell Hill Junior School

THE BOMB

Me and my friend found a bomb yesterday,
It was in the middle of the road.
I was so scared and terrified,
I thought it was going to explode.

Now we see the funny side of it,
It was all a fraud you know.
Guess what?
Yesterday, we thought we were going abroad.

Emily Young (9)
Muswell Hill Junior School

SKELETON ESCAPE

I am a skeleton.
I live in the Natural History Museum.
Every night me and my friends try to escape.
But we never seem to be able to.
We have secret tunnels hidden behind paintings.
But most of them lead to dead ends.
We are trying to find one that leads outside
So we can go out on Hallowe'en and scare everybody.
We will chase them out of town,
And throw rotten cheese at everyone.
We found the tunnel that leads out and escaped.
It was Hallowe'en.
We threw rotten cheese
And left banana skins about.

Christopher Preston (8)
Muswell Hill Junior School

MOUSE

The mouse is walking down the street
Walking fast in the heat
I play football in the house
But when I see that funny mouse
Crawl in that hole
Just like a mole
I think mice are just so cool
They're not like dogs, they don't drool!

Matthew Dudson-Green (9)
Muswell Hill Junior School

THE HOSPITAL

My hospital has a skeleton in it
I think it's going to eat me up.
When I was going to bed
I looked across the road into the hospital.
There were lights shining
Out of the hospital.
'Mum, Mum!'
'What?'
'Look at the hospital.'
'Oh yer, let's call the police.'
'OK.'
The police went to the hospital.
When they got in it was quiet.
When I went to my hospital
I looked at the skeleton.
It opened its jaw and moved its mouth.
The next day I went to the hospital again.
The skeleton was gone.

Azania Stewart (9)
Muswell Hill Junior School

THE LEOPARD

Gentle eyes and soft whiskers.
Big spots, little spots, all different sizes.
In beauty competitions he always wins the prizes.
Padding through the jungle floor
All the animals bow as the jungle lord passes.
As he looks up at a tree and jumps up and just lies there in the sun.
The animal of grace purrs and falls asleep.

Saskia Freemantle (10)
Muswell Hill Junior School

THE SKELETON

I am a skeleton.
I stand in the corner of the room.
Lots of interesting people come in the room.
They stare at me and I stare back.
Other skeletons are hanging on the walls.
When everyone has gone and turned off the light
We have a party
All night long till six o'clock.
At six o'clock the people come in.
Then they stare at me again for a day.
I am delighted when the light goes out.
We have another party.

Charlie Miller (8)
Muswell Hill Junior School

THE WIND

The wind is a powerful thing,
fierce and strong and loud.
It pulls the washing round the line
which turns and tangles round.
It rattles at your window.
It cries all through the night.
When you're trying to sleep it comes
knocking at your window in spite
calling 'Let me in! Let me in! Let me in!'

Katie Durka (9)
Muswell Hill Junior School

WIND BLOWS DAMAGE

W ind, you are annoying when
I cy gusts of you come through the window.
N othing wails as much as you!
D o you really bite and slice?

B lustery wind, if only you would blow away!
L ovely weather is sunshine, not wind.
O f all weather you're one of the worst.
W ind comes in autumn to blow leaves off trees
S trong and fierce. That's not now.

D o you just come in autumn? No.
A big wind I would hate much more,
M aybe I could make friends with you.
A nother wind would be nice for you. If you
G o away, maybe I would be sad.
E lectricity kills. Not you.

Clara Chinnery (9)
Muswell Hill Junior School

A SKELETON

I'm a skeleton.
I've got no face.
No hair.
I feel I'm not there.
Except for when they run and hide in fear.
And then I cry and cry.
I feel so cold and glum.
I've got no friends.

Alex Jones (8)
Muswell Hill Junior School

PANCAKES!

First you get the sticky syrup
Dash it on a plate
Sitting at the table shouting,
'I want my pancake!'

The first one goes
right down in my tummy,
Mmmm, yummy, yummy.

I flipped the second
then it fell
And I think it's gone to . . .
pancake hell!

Ben Hounam (8)
Muswell Hill Junior School

THE WIND

The wind is fierce and fun.
It's got its own talents.
Now it's playing with the washing line.
Dad's gone to stop it but now he's blown away,
As he hangs on the fence for dear life,
My brother thinks it's funny.
But I'm not laughing.
It's pulling at the street lights.
It's pushing at the trees.
When will it stop?
Nobody knows.

Farhang Shahidi (9)
Muswell Hill Junior School

MAN U

United are the only team
Every night I dream and dream
That Man United hold the cup
And Arsenal are the runners-up.

There's only one man
He's Andy Cole
When he gets the ball
He scores a goal.

Man U fight another day
Here's what Arsenal had to say
'Giggs tormented us, so did Cole
But Sheringham scored a cracking goal.'

Kerim Ozkolaci (8)
Muswell Hill Junior School

THE WIND

The wind howls, wails and rattles.
It rips washing lines down.
The biting, slicing wind.
It blows you over.
It swooshes round and round and round.
It's so sudden it makes the windows rattle.
The big big gusts of wind
Make my eyes water.

Nicholas Rance (8)
Muswell Hill Junior School

THE CHEETAH

The cheetah runs swiftly through the grass.
He runs over stumps and past moving things.
He jumps over ponds and lakes.
He carries animals on his back
And takes them where they're going.
He is browny-yellow and has black spots.
He runs over the meadows
Like a Concorde at full speed.
He is the fastest runner in the world.
He is part of the cat family.
He jumps like a crystal rock.
He is happy and sad and never bad.
The fastest runner in the world.

Hannah Baldock (9)
Muswell Hill Junior School

THE WIND

The tins are rattling.
The cat is moaning.
The wind is blowing under my bed covers.
My legs are shivering.
My feet have gone numb but the night goes on.
I feel my soft furry cat keeping my feet warm.
Woooo. There's a ghost in my room.
My cat comes higher up my bed.
I hold it tight and wish the night would finish.

Athena Tasou (9)
Muswell Hill Junior School

OVER THE MOON

Boarding rocket ready for take-off
Setting control pad to 'on'
Settling down
Going through a list of things
Hoping they are all there
Blankets, check; rugs, check;
And all sorts of food
Now it really is time for take-off
Whizzing out of the world's atmosphere
And into deep dark space
Stars glinting like diamonds everywhere
Spinning past Jupiter
Spinning past Mars
Sliding down the Milky Way
And up to the Moon.

Georgina Stevens (8)
Muswell Hill Junior School

MY BEST FRIEND

My best friend is good to me.
My best friend plays with me
when I am lonely.
My best friend makes me happy
when I get hurt.
My best friend has blonde hair.
My best friend says
'Cheer up' when I am sad.

Nancy Breen (9)
Muswell Hill Junior School

THE TIGER

The tiger slips silently through the night,
Not making a single sound.
He creeps along the shadowy ground,
Searching for his prey.

He climbs a tall, tall tree,
And looks to see if there's anything moving in sight.
There doesn't seem to be anything, but there is,
A small creature in the distance.

He gets down from the tree with great care,
He doesn't want to spoil it now,
And pads up to a bush near his prey.
He crouches in the long grass, and
waits . . .

Suddenly he pounces,
And that is the end.

Jessica Thompson (9)
Muswell Hill Junior School

DECEMBER

December's charming children
know how to get their way.
They try so hard they always win
And make you laugh each day.
They're charmed with a turquoise birthstone
As blue as the sea below,
Like the clown fish
Like the sky
And they're never looking low.

Georgina Charalambous (9)
Muswell Hill Junior School

SEASONS

Spring
    I like the season of spring
    The birds singing in the trees
    Happily making their cosy nests
    The buds are growing into leaves
    Fresh blossom smelling sweet
    The rain falls in crystal drops
    Sun shines with warm rays
    They come together to make a rainbow
    Hedgehogs come out of their winter sleep.

Summer
    I like the season of summer
    The sun shines so nice and bright
    I laugh and run under the sun
    We go to the park and go to the pool
    We go to places that are cool
    We have so much fun in the sun.

Autumn
    I like the season of autumn
    The leaves go all brown and crunchy
    Autumn is all brown and dull and dark
    Like night-time
    It's dark and so chilly
    It's cold and rainy
    That's the nice thing about autumn.

Winter
    I like the season of winter
    It's cold and fresh like winter snow
    I like the snow, you run and jump
    In the cold white snow
    Go to the mountain where it's colder
    Scream, hear your echo
    Build an igloo, get inside
    Before you freeze to death.

Megan Atkinson (8)
Muswell Hill Junior School

FOOD GLORIOUS FOOD

All I can think about is food, glorious food.
Piles of jelly and toffees, fruit pastels
and mint ice-cream with nuts and cherries.
When I wake up in the morning
my tummy says it's time for morning breakfast.
What I have for breakfast is,
ice-cream, Frosties, pancakes
and lots of other things
and then I have to go to boring school.
I *hate* it because all we ever do is maths.
To keep me going I have tons of sweets
inside my desk.
I never got home because I burst.
I didn't care because in heaven
there is more food than you could put in your mouth.

Sam Barrett Binney (9)
Muswell Hill Junior School

THE AMAZING TV

I wake up one morning with my brain bust
I shake my head clear, I walk into the living room
I sit on the couch switching the TV on
I am a couch potato
Staring at this little screen
I had never heard of TV
Ever since I discovered this
I have watched it every day.

The most amazing thing is
            TV.

George Newton (9)
Muswell Hill Junior School

FEATHERS

They drift slowly from side to side
falling on the ground trying to hide.
Every bird has them,
feathers that blow in the wind.
I don't think they would mind
if one of their feathers from behind
fell off.
The people who find them,
lovely pretty feathers,
are quite a lucky few.
I was wondering if one
could be you.

Janine Houston (8)
Muswell Hill Junior School

GOLDEN LION TAMARIN MONKEYS

Jumping across from tree to tree,
Golden Lion Tamarin monkeys are hard to see,

Golden manes, beautiful and shiny,
Golden Lion Tamarin monkeys are so tiny,

Long sleek bodies, twist and turn,
Their colour looks like they will start to burn.

I love them!

Romaine Louise Graham (8)
Muswell Hill Junior School

FOOTBALL GAMES

Walking down the tunnel, hearing the crowds cheer,
Autograph books at the ready,
Oh please sir!
It's edging nearer, nearer by the minute,
The crowd's roar comes even closer,
There it is, we've come out!
The game has started,
Tensions grow up,
But we've gone out now.
It's half-time, we're losing 1-0.
Out we come at the beginning of the second half,
Ten minutes later . . . *hurrah* we've scored.
5,4,3,2 and 1 - *pheep*
and it's all over.

Freddie Burgess (8)
Muswell Hill Junior School

MAKE THE MOST OF A SUNNY DAY

Make the most of a sunny day,
Nag your parents to take you away,
Maybe on a picnic,
Maybe to the park,
If you nag them really hard,
They might take you to see a shark.

Make the most of a sunny day,
It might be your dream come true.

Phoebe Fullbrook (8)
Muswell Hill Junior School

The Sunset

The sun shines on the glittering water,
Making it pink, orange and welcoming,
Friendly it beckons to you, asking,
It makes you feel cheerful inside,
You can hear the waves lapping together,
Murmuring in whispers,
Calm and peaceful
That's what I like.
The orange, red, pink and yellow sunset
Lights up the sky,
Like a flickering candle,
I could stand there forever, just looking at the sunset,
It was quiet too, so quiet you could hear a needle drop,
On the bottom of the ocean floor,
Where pearls and corals lie,
That's what I like.
The glistening grass is moist as I sit down,
My hand brushes against a stone,
Smooth and cold,
Slender and orangey in the light,
Then complete darkness overtakes me.

Elisabeth Salverda (9)
Muswell Hill Junior School

Getting To Sleep

I *hate* getting to sleep!

There are monsters in my bed,
There are thoughts going round my head,
I get all hot and kick the covers off,
Then I lose my toy,
        I pull the covers back on,

I *hate* getting to sleep!

I'm worried about nightmares,
I'm worried about the next day,
I hear Mum and Dad having a great time
        with friends downstairs,

I *hate* getting to sleep!

Francesca Wickers (9)
Muswell Hill Junior School

THE DOG IN THE WIND

The dog, a calm animal in a way

Poor thing on the streets, its hair blowing in the wind
poor thing looking for a person loving and caring
a sad female getting damp and wet
poor thing cold and hungry, no one for a friend.
A loving pet trapped in the rain
she is sad, unloved and been nothing to anyone
no one minds if she's on the streets
no one wants her.

They don't care, they've just got other pets to care for.
The poor thing could die
I'd like to have a dog
Its hair is still blowing in the wind
Its sad little eyes staring at me begging for help.
I feel horrible, I can't help it.

The dog must be wishing its owner was nicer by now.

Nuha Ham (9)
Muswell Hill Junior School

THE YUMMY SCRUMMY LUNCH BOX

A nice way to start
is a jam tart.
A litre of Pepsi, let's have a slurp.
Another litre of cola
I need to burp.
May I have a cream cake please?
I will give you all my cheese.
Please may I have your fromage frais?
Go on, put it on my tray.
May I swap my lovely mango
for a little of your Tango?
Now I have swapped all my food and cake,
what will you swap
for my *tummy ache?*

Michael Botsford (9)
Muswell Hill Junior School

I'M NOT SLEEPY

'Honest mum, I'm not sleepy,
don't send me to bed.
P..p..please mum, I'm not sleepy,
don't send me to bed.
I can watch this, I'm not sleepy,
don't send me to bed.
Five more minutes, I'm not sleepy,
don't send me to bed.'
Yawn . . .
'Mum, I'm not sleepy,
don't send me to bed'
Zzzzzzzz.

Jason Bond (9)
Muswell Hill Junior School

AUTUMN SPIDERS

From tree to tree spiders on their sparkling
webs go to and fro catching their prey like flies
and wasps.
Their magnificent figures on their glittering
webs on rainy days look like a string of
diamonds.
Hanging from the sky some spiders can bite.
It is very painful.
Sometimes blood can appear.
You can get all types of spiders, tall and
small.
But they are lovely.

Jonathan Winnington (9)
Muswell Hill Junior School

MY MUM

My mum is sweet
Sweet as a rose
I've tasted sugar,
But I bet you are
Sweeter than any rose
In the world
She cooks every day,
Beans, pasta and rice.
Always smiles,
Time by time
I love my mum.

Jazmine Cox (8)
North Harringay Junior School

SPLISHING AND SPLASHING

I hate rain
Splishing and splashing.

I hate when it rains
Splishing and splashing.

I hate rain
Splishing and splashing
When it rains I didn't want to go outside
Splishing and splashing.

Rain, rain I don't like rain.
Splishing and splashing.

Rain, rain go to Spain
Where you're needed
You're really a pain.
Splishing and splashing.

Esaa Choudury (7)
North Harringay Junior School

SPRING

S pring is my favourite season.
P oppies bloom in the spring.
R aspberries are juicier in the spring.
I   ce-creams are cooler in the spring.
N etball is played more in spring.
G eese lay eggs in spring.

Joe Botham (9)
North Harringay Junior School

I HATE RAIN

I hate rain
Jumping and splashing.
My shoes are wet
Jumping and splashing.
Jodie kicks water at me
Jumping and splashing.
Someone pushes me in a puddle
Jumping and splashing.
I go home it stops raining
Jumping and splashing.
Finally I got home
Jumping and splashing.
My mum wants me to go down the shop
Jumping and splashing.
I get outside
Jumping and splashing.
It starts raining again
Jumping and splashing.

Jade Hare (8)
North Harringay Junior School

SUMMER

S un, bright, light.
U p in the sky shining bright.
M emories of the bright sun.
M aking the world light up.
E lephants pulling down trees in North Africa
      in summer.
R ising up from the water.

Chantelle Rhone (9)
North Harringay Junior School

SUMMER POEM

S ummer is hot and bright lots of light too
   When you go to parties it is fun.
U ntil the winter comes it is very hot
   you can play with a pot.
M ore swimming pools are open and you can swim,
M y dog can play and swim and have lots of fun,
E ven I can play on a horse so it's hot and fun,
R easons for me liking summer is it is hot and fun.

Lauren Hooper (9)
North Harringay Junior School

SUMMER POEM

S ummer is lovely nice and boiling.
U nder the sea where you can see.
M agnificent tennis on the court.
M ummy, Mummy it's so hot.
E verywhere is boiling it's so hot.
R adical, radical I want to do it again.

Philippe Kane (9)
North Harringay Junior School

SPRING BEAUTY

S pring is so wonderful you can't leave the field you are in,
P ansies, daisies, daffodils, nice green grass,
R inging in your ears are the bleats of little lambs,
I n your vision of view is the beautifulness of spring,
N o wars, nothing to disturb the peace,
G oing on to summer, a holiday ahead for you.

Padraig Anderson (8)
North Harringay Junior School

SPRING

S pring is coming everyone is happy.
P aper is wasting everyone is sad
   and the men were cutting trees.
R iver is bright shining with the light.
I n and out the horses came, to find a name
N ow the traffic is crying because
   he cannot find a fame name.
G rape is lovely in spring so everyone buys it.

Guilherme Reis (9)
North Harringay Junior School

SPRING POEM

S ummertime fun, that's my name, come with me and
P lay the game.
R eady to play the game racing down the hill,
I ce-cream on me with all my will.
N ice hot day on the hill.
G et more juice that's a deal.

Tarik Azuzoglu (9)
North Harringay Junior School

SUMMER

S ummer, beautiful bright sunshine.
U p in the sky, bright sun.
M ountains nice and light.
M outh-watering melon has been picked from the sun.
E arly in the morning I wake up and see the sun.
R eally bright sunlight, oh no, forgetting to go to the beach.

Runeyda Bacak (9)
North Harringay Junior School

MY SHADOW

She follows me around wherever I go,
She stays beside me attached to my toe.
I forget about her deep in the night,
And when I see her she gives me a fright.

My shadow is with me all of the time,
Following each action as a mime.
She seems like my family or my friend,
I wonder if our friendship will ever end.

She comes out especially on sunny days,
She copies and knows every one of my ways.
Everyone has a shadow not just me,
And from my shadow I cannot flee.

Rachel Hedley (10)
Queenswell Junior School

A FEAR

A fear is when you get butterflies
With only a pencil and eraser,
You're not alone.
Half way through the test
You hear a silent tick,
You hear the pencil on the paper scribbling away,
You hear the eraser scrubbing the paper in dismay.
Then finally you hear the bell
It could be a fire drill,
Or the end of the test.
I hope I passed,
I tried my best.

Alex Evans (11)
Queenswell Junior School

THE POEM

A poem is just like a chameleon
It can change colour, just like a poem can change a mood
Some are sad, some are happy
Whilst some are hilarious.
A chameleon can be white, maybe black
At other times it can be red
It can be about life, the cosmos
Whether there is life on Mars or not
It can be about anything, anything one desires
Some are just like games of 'Who am I?'
Where the poet wants to hide something,
Which in fact can only be seen if you look at the way it's written
Whilst others are a mystery in themselves,
Throwing the reader questions, but never answers.
Some are about the hills, mountainside,
Creating pictures in the reader's mind that are so vivid
That it feels as if you can reach out and enter this 'Land'
Others are funny, yet in a sense solemn.
But all poems have one thing in common
It's not their mood, not the thing they are describing
Not even the picture that they create:
It's the way it's written.
Using words that make you think:
Is this ever possible?

Maciek Gmerek (11)
Queenswell Junior School

SILVER AND GOLD

Silver shine
The sky's not mine
Quarter moon
Comes too soon
Half moon
Almost lost
Three quarter moon
Amongst the frost
Comes too soon
The full moon
Time for crazy acts
Not for facts
At harvest
Twenty-four carat
Farmers invest
Gold is where you're at.

Rebecca Casey (10)
Queenswell Junior School

THE ZOO

Off to the zoo we went, where we saw,
Pheasants, chickens and peacocks galore,
Zebras, elephants, rhinos too
All in the same place at the zoo.

Snakes and lizards, moths and toads,
We ate crisps and biscuits loads and loads.
The man in the hat was feeding the bears
The zebras and wolves the rabbits and hares.

The seals were swimming, the penguins were diving
The animal life in the zoo was thriving.
Round the cages up the path
Then we saw the monkeys, they made us laugh.

Round the corner we came to the lions' cage
The cheetahs growled, the leopards purred,
The lions roared with rage.
Owls that hoot, cows that moo
That was my first time at the zoo.

Emma Rowbotham (10)
Queenswell Junior School

FEAR

A sudden shudder.
I feel an itch.
It's making the lights go out.
I feel the pressure mounting.
I'm all alone.
Been standing here for minutes,
But it seems like hours.
A creak at the door.
It's entering the room.
I call out,
But still silence and darkness.
Sweating now.
Total panic.
Immense fear.
It's up my leg.
Further up,
Towards my waist
And, and, and . . .

Aran Kemal (11)
Queenswell Junior School

WHAT'S THAT NOISE?

It's dark at night,
I'm all alone,
There's all these creeping noises, is someone
coming to get me?
No it's just my imagination . . . it's just my imagination.
I'll just go to sleep, but what if someone gets me when I'm asleep.
I'm so scared.
Should I go to my parents' room?
No it's too far.
It's scary on my own.
I try to shout - but nothing comes out.
Oh no,
It's coming closer it's . . . it's . . . it's
O' boy it's just my dog Sam with his bone.

Sharon-Louise Griffiths (10)
Queenswell Junior School

MYSTERIOUS WIND

Whenever I hear the howling cry,
The plants,
The trees are swaying by.
Crunchy leaves blow away,
It's not that bad during the day.

At night I hear the ghostly sound,
I hope it'll head homely bound.
The sound I hear,
Is coming near,
Near enough to scare me clear.

The tapping sound is near the door,
The vibration slowly hits the floor.
The breeze is coming near to me,
It's chilling like the ice cold sea!

The sound I hear is just the wind,
Rushing out,
And swirling in.

Shirin Sheibani (10)
Queenswell Junior School

THE POND AT WINTER

It is winter now.
There are benches by the pond.
It is in the park.

Everything is calm.
There are pigeons by the pond.
Ducks are in the pond.

The pond is oval.
The water looks very cold.
Rushes in the pond.

A path surrounds it.
There is no one near the pond.
The birds are alone.

There is a footpath.
Path goes half way across the pond.
Pillars surround it.

The pond is lovely.
I have known it all my life.
The pond at winter.

Daniel Newby (11)
Queenswell Junior School

FEAR

I am watching TV
There is a knock
Who is it?
What is it?

All the lights go off
My heart is beating faster
Then the TV screen goes blank
The door opens

It takes a shot
It misses
My dad comes down with a gun
He shoots a bullet
He dies
Phew.

Poonit Depala (10)
Queenswell Junior School

TREES

Now it's spring, it's time to grow,
Brightly blossomed, what a show,
Flowers come out for all to see,
To be enjoyed by you and me.

Now it's summer, the sun's full out
Children play, sing and shout,
Under the tree, in the cool shade,
The picnic's out, perfectly laid.

Now it's autumn, the leaves are rust,
Flowers and leaves turn to dust,
Acorns and conkers fall to the ground,
In a heap, forming a mound.

Now it's winter, everything sleeps,
Hedgehogs hiding, squirrels peep,
The landscape's quiet, all is bleak,
Winter folds itself in the deep.

Lucy Hershon (10)
Queenswell Junior School

LIGHTNING

The night is dark
It's cold outside
The rain is pouring down
From the lightning I hide

As the lightning strikes
I feel a shiver
Down my spine
I start to quiver

The lightning shoots down from the sky
At the speed of light
It comes down as a spark
And gives me an awful fright.

Elmaz Hussein (10)
Queenswell Junior School

EVERYTHING ON ITS WAY DOWN

Outside the wind howls,
it crashes into the windows.
The doors begin to
open and slam shut,
The windows throw out
threatening creaks as
the roof starts to
feel uncomfortable.
Leafless trees throw
themselves about
while things start
to seem dreadful.
The noise gets
louder then *crack*
what's that?
The chimney's on its
way down.
One down lots more to go
shouts the bullying wind.
The town is lit up
with house lights on,
everyone is awake.

Helen Myer (10)
Queenswell Junior School

SEASONS

Winter brings ice and snow,
Skating and sledging we can go.
Flowers and trees are all asleep,
To match our mood the scene is bleak.

Spring is a time when all awakes,
We cut the lawn and mend the gates.
Everything seems fresh and new,
The sun is out, the sky is blue.

Summer days are lazy and long,
To the beach the crowds do throng.
Swimming in the shimmering sea,
Worries are forgotten, everyone is carefree.

Autumn trees all around,
Shedding leaves golden brown.
Animals settle down to rest,
Birds migrate and leave their nest.

Summer, autumn, winter, spring,
Each one shows a different thing.
Throughout the twelve months of the year,
We always know they will be here.

Hannah Saffer (10)
Queenswell Junior School

THE NIGHT

Whenever the moon and stars are set,
Whenever the clouds are high,
I glare above the dark misty houses,
And admire the startling sky.

Soon after the thunder strikes,
Down my spine runs a shiver,
The sound of the wind moaning,
Makes my body quiver.

I hear the rustling of the leaves,
Moreover the stars light,
I hear the crying of the wind,
However, appreciate the bright, lustre winter night.

I stroll along the dark, dark street,
And look down at me,
My shadow follows me everywhere,
It gives me the creeps to see.

As the night drags on slowly,
The burning gas glows up high,
As I stare up at the moon,
Everything turns so dark, Why?

Amy Cordell (11)
Queenswell Junior School

THE MOUSE

The mouse came out its hiding place,
He ran across the room at pace.
To where his nose had sensed the smell,
Coming from the biscuit barrel.

He climbed the wall with the greatest of ease,
And past the kitchen drawer's keys.
And there upon the shelf it stood,
The mouse's feast, it smelt so good.

He ran towards it, his mouth open wide,
Drooling at the meal inside.
He found a way to climb the side,
He lifted the lid and peeked inside.

He dived in and began to eat,
And enjoyed his great feat.
In biscuit he was soon caked,
He ate until his tummy ached.

Then the mouse got up and looked around,
Not a crumb nor biscuit to be found.
He then discovered with a shout,
That he was too big and couldn't get out.

He tried and tried but all in vain,
He couldn't escape, it was just a pain.
The mouse sat down and began to weep,
The moral is, 'Look before you leap!'

Daniel Smith (11)
Queenswell Junior School

BIG AND SMALL

As big as a log,
as small as a frog.
As big as a house,
as small as a louse.
As big as a tree,
as small as me.
As big as a bus,
as small as us.
As big as an eagle,
as small as a Pringle.
As big as a lollipop,
as small as a raindrop.
As big as a moor,
as small as a door.
As big as a boat,
as small as a goat.
As big as a cat,
as small as a rat.

Sarah-Ann McGinn (9)
St Francis De Sales Junior School

HARD AND SOFT

As hard as my head,
As soft as my bed.
As hard as a case,
As soft as my face.
As hard as an ice rink,
As soft as an ink.
As hard as a clock,
As soft as my sock.

Jennifer Ihekweme (8)
St Francis De Sales Junior School

BIG/SMALL

As big as an elephant stamping on the street.
As small as a brown ant trying to get around.
As big as a very large blue bathroom.
As small as yukky yellow candy.
As big as a green flowery hill park.
As small as a little newborn yellow chick.
As big as a huge watery pop star's swimming pool.
As small as a green pea in a large pot.
As big as a smooth school table.
As small as a baby slithering snake.
As big as a fierce brown bear.
As small as Rachel's tiny gold earrings.
As big as James O's fat pencil case.

Siobhan O'Doherty (10)
St Francis De Sales Junior School

FOOD

Choppy chives checking out the chips
Happy hamburgers hurting herds of heifers
Pepperoni pizzas partying with soda pop
Big barbecue burgers burnt on buns
Succulent steak sizzling on a side plate
Tasty turkey tapping on the trifle
Smoky salmon singing on the spoon
Jammy jelly jumping in the jam
Ripping rice rich and royal
Chinese chicken chosen to cook a cod
Piercing hot pies pushing in the pot.

Derek Oppong (10)
St Francis De Sales Junior School

SHOCK FOR A CROC

The sun shone down on his long nose,
As from the river his body rose.
His teeth were sharp and shaped like knives,
This crocodile king with many wives.

Today he'd made plans to grab a child,
A nice cuddly one, so meek and mild.
He didn't care how the child would feel,
He wanted one for his meal.

He waddled through the jungle thick,
And came to the village to take his pick.
But the monkey had warned them in advance,
They were waiting for him with knives and lance.

They cornered him into a net,
'We'll take care of you, you're no pet!'
And as they pierced him with a spear,
Down his nose ran a crocodile tear.

David Mulcahy (10)
St Francis De Sales Junior School

SIMILE POEM

As sharp as a knife
As terrible as bloody Mary
As fast as a car
As hot as a volcano
As grumpy as Henry VIII
As dirty as mud
As fat as Henry VIII.

Damien Cunningham (10)
St Francis De Sales Junior School

IN MY CLASS

First in school, of course it's Paul,
Looking for the moon is Jamie Noone,
Pouncing like a panther is Samantha,
Being a good carer is Sarah,
The one that hates woodlice, is of course Kimberley Pryce.
This girl has a fan, the name is Stacey Ann,
She laid her work out nice and neat, Alisha Jade you'd love to meet,
She drinks a lot of lemonade, it can't be anyone but Sinead,
In the wet and windy gale, the only one out was Dale.
If you look for someone merry, you will always find Kerri,
There'll always be attention, with Mrs Hutchinson.

Melanie Socrates (7)
St Francis De Sales Junior School

ABOUT ME

Always nice
Never being nasty
Nice hair style
Ever friendly

My age is 10
Able to dance
Really chatty
I like chocolate cake
Every day.

Anne Marie Holleran (10)
St Francis De Sales Junior School

MY PET MONSTER

I know a monster who's green and mean,
He has big green eyes he loves apple pies,
He's quite a friendly chap,
He has a little red cap,
He has a very long tail,
Once he ate a snail!
He has lots of big red spots,
He loves to go to the shops,
He has four fingers on his hands,
He loves to listen to pop bands,
He lives in a bin,
He's got an earring!
So if you see a big green monster
With red spots *'scream!'*

Bonnie Kennedy (10)
St Francis De Sales Junior School

MY DREAM

There I was lying in my bed,
Cuddling and kissing my little friend Ted,
With a clat and a clatter
A dream washed through my head.

Here I was going mad,
Bits were happy, bits were sad,
Cindy Crawford and all the girls
This must be the best dream of
all the worlds.

Scott Waldron (9)
St Francis De Sales Junior School

MY PET WHALE

My pet whale,
looks quite pale.
My pet whale,
has a female friend.
He has a kind heart,
and likes eating tart.
He wakes at eight,
and hates it when I'm late.
Every year he drinks a cup of beer,
which makes him fight, like Shakespeare.

Hoa Le (9)
St Francis De Sales Junior School

HARD AND SOFT

As hard as a block,
As soft as a sock.
As hard as a wall,
As soft as a ball.
As soft as Flubber,
As hard as a hammer.
As soft as foam,
As hard as a microphone.
As soft as a cake
Which you can bake.
Please be nice and give me a slice.

Jean-Paul Willie (9)
St Francis De Sales Junior School

SCARY AND FRIENDLY

As scary as a ghost,
As friendly as me.
As scary as a vampire,
As friendly as a bee.
As scary as a spook,
As friendly as Linda.
As scary as a ghost book,
As friendly as a bird.
As scary as a devil,
As friendly as a friend.
As scary as a Celt,
As friendly as a parent.

Tom Kennedy (9)
St Francis De Sales Junior School

FAST AND SLOW

As fast as a cheetah,
As slow as a turtle,
As fast as a car,
As slow as a worm.

As fast as a runner,
As slow as a snail,
As fast as a hare,
As slow as a snake,
As fast as a motorbike
As slow as a kite.

Fiona Boateng (8)
St Francis De Sales Junior School

HARD AND SOFT

As hard as a rock,
As soft as a pillow,
As hard as a brick,
As soft as sugar,
As hard as a ruler,
As soft as wool,
As hard as a computer,
As soft as a hairband,
As hard as a table,
As soft as paper,
As hard as a highlighter,
As soft as skin,
As hard as a brick,
As soft as a baby chick.

Shauna Small (8)
St Francis De Sales Junior School

BIG AND SMALL

As big as my brother,
As small as me,
As big as a crane,
As small as a cane.

As big as the giant as little as me,
As big as a house as small as a mouse,
As big as a tree and as little as me.

Samuel Badu-Antwi
St Francis De Sales Junior School

FRUIT AND VEGETABLES

An apple is agreeable, amazing and attractive and
also acceptable
Bananas are beautiful totally not bitter,
Carrots are crunchy, cheap and chewy,
Dates are delicious, David likes them
Eggs are not enormous but very exiguous
They're very nice to eat 'cos they're excellent.
A fig is fabulous, it is always fresh
It has a lot of fluid and is very flavoursome.
Grapes are gorgeous, grand and good.
They can be green. They can be food.
A hip is heavenly and not that hairy.
It's not humongous and not harmonious.
But Indian mangoes are incredible and irresistible.
Jack fruits are sometimes juicy, they're not all jammy.

Jenny Cachero (10)
St Francis De Sales Junior School

CIRCUS

The clumsy clowns charged to the centre of the circus.
The athletic acrobatics amazed the audience.
Eight enormous elephants each have eighteen eyes.
Seven sea-lions smile as they show off.
The jugglers jumped as they juggled with joy.
The terrifying tigers threatened to tear up the
teenagers with their teeth.
The leaping lions looked at the lovely ladies and
licked their lips.
The disco dancers danced till they dropped.

Christopher Noone (10)
St Francis De Sales Junior School

MY EMBARRASSING FAMILY

I have an embarrassing family,
because they always are acting madly.
There's my nan called Pintops,
who sings Firestarter in the shops.
My granpa with the knowledge,
but at 85 still in college.
My mum, Sue, who looks like a punk,
and thinks Keith in the Prodigy is a real hunk.
Next is my dad who acts like a king,
shows off to the girls, saying check out my new ring.
Then there's my brother who thinks he's cool,
I think that's probably why he got kicked out of school.
Tosha's my sister who is a hippy,
she's the sort of person who'd get married to a tree.
My uncle Jack who loves a treat,
and if I don't give him one he'll give me a beating.
My aunt Mabel snores so loud,
that when I look out of the window I see a crowd.
As for me I'm as normal as can be,
but I have an embarrassing family.

Vanessa Adjei (10)
St Francis De Sales Junior School

CIRCUS

A clumsy clown charged around the circus.
Artistic acrobats did their annoying act.
Eight elephants began to eat enormous eggs.
Running right ringmasters, ran around the ring.
A few funny fat figures were the funniest for five days.

Patrick Wilson (10)
St Francis De Sales Junior School

SOFT AND HARD

As soft as a rabbit,
As hard as a rock,
As soft as a towel,
As hard as a clock.

As soft as my bed,
As hard as my head,
As soft as a hare,
As hard as a chair.

As soft as a pillow,
As hard as a tin,
As soft as a cloud,
As hard as a bin.

Linda Ohemeng (9)
St Francis De Sales Junior School

THE ZOO

One wild wacky wallaby
Two terrapins terribly tired
Three tarantulas eat tadpoles
Four fish fighting
Five fat frogs
Six slimy slugs
Seven skinny sharks
Eight anteaters
Nine nice newts.

Eugene Nicolaou (10)
St Francis De Sales Junior School

DEAN THE BULLY MACHINE

Dean was very keen to be mean.
With a glint in his eye he could eat your pork pie.
With a twitch of his nose he could steal your clothes.

Dressed up in his rags he chatted up a girl called Mags.
'How about a date' said Dean
'You must be joking' said Mags
'I'd rather help my mum carry her shopping bags'

Dean stepped into the playground with
An astonishingly big greyhound.
The children huddled for protection
This monster dog showed no affection.
Scruffy coat and teeth were yellow.
Dean the bully was an awful fellow.

Niall Malone (10)
St Francis De Sales Junior School

MY OWN SIMILE POEM

As small as a tiny little mouse,
As big as a six storey house.
As small as a pea in a pod,
As big as the love of our Father God.
As small as the tiniest eye of a needle,
As big as a giant among all people.
As small as the pupil of my eye,
As big as the whole of the clouds and the sky.

Rachel Johnson (9)
St Francis De Sales Junior School

MY FAVOURITE FOOD

For breakfast I have pickled onions
and ice-cream on the top
but maybe that is far too much
and so disgusting is . . .
the lunch I have straight after that,
it is so quite disgusting I can't believe my eyes,
it's sort of like a mixture.
I have it every time.
It is the mix of bacon and sausage
washed down by a bar of soap
and orange juice with milk,
For dinner it's a different matter
there's fish, liver and also a Smartie tube
all mixed with spaghetti sauce
I love it very much.
For supper when I'm going to bed,
(this might seem pretty strange)
a coffee and sugar sandwich
and to finish off
coleslaw and beetroot mixed up
with ravioli in tomato sauce.
(Yum Yum!)

Stacie Ravenor (10)
St Francis De Sales Junior School

FOOD

Mischievous Matthew munched McVities.
An African alligator ate an animal's Adam's apple.
Silly Sally sucked some satsumas.
Tasting Tommy tempted Tony to try the tarts.
Cookery Charlie changed chocolates' complexion.

James Onumonu (10)
St Francis De Sales Junior School

ROLLER-SKATING

R is for roller-skating slowly down the hills.
O is for roller-skating on your own roller-skates.
L is for looking where you're going when you're roller-skating.
L is to look at your roller-skates.
E is to watch where you're going with your eyes.
R is for roller-skating in a ring.
S is for singing while you're roller-skating.
K is for bending your knees while roller-skating.
A is for getting all of your friends.
T is for giving people tips on roller-skating.
I is for you not to roller-skate all day or you get ill.
N is for roller-skating all night.
G is for getting your grip ready to roller-skate.

Obiechina Emodi-Okechukwu (9)
St Francis De Sales Junior School

KEVIN'S LIFE

A boy called Kevin was eleven,
two years ago.
He likes drinking beer even though
he's not allowed.
Kevin thought he was cool,
but everyone at school
Thought he was a fool.
Kevin saw a bug on the floor
but his teacher gave him a big hug.
Kevin had a dog and a frog.
Kevin got ill,
But then he died.

Sinead Folan (10)
St Francis De Sales Junior School

THE CRAZY WEDDING

I've been invited to a lousy wedding,
Of barmy Auntie Lou and Uncle Jim,
He's going to dress in red and bring a broom,
I've never ever known such a crazy groom.
He was eight hours late and went to the wrong church,
Poor Auntie Lou just waited in the lurch,
She couldn't wait any longer and put on the ring,
And jumped on the altar and danced the Highland fling.
At midnight we were dozing in our seats,
Then we felt an air of wind and heat,
It was only Uncle Jim opening the door,
And with these words he threw himself on the floor,
'Oh dear Louie, my dear sweetheart,
Please forgive me with all your heart,'
We all stared at him and laughed and grinned,
They kissed each other and we sang hymns.
The wedding cake was strangely blue,
And it was made by you know who,
We danced all night to rock 'n' roll,
Until we dropped and sleep-walked home.

Antonia Pisano (10)
St Francis De Sales Junior School

THE FARM

Pink pigs eating,
yellow chicks learning to walk,
white sheep playing,
brown cows munching grass,
a black sheep dog running about,
that's what's on the farm.

Angela Braganza (9)
St Francis De Sales Junior School

Taste Of Winter

Snow falls on the ground,
Thick the snow goes on,
Children play with snow.
Have snowball fights and make snowmen.

I ride on a sledge,
Go skiing with friends,
And I get a red nose,
Though I dress in warm clothes.

The snow crunches when you walk,
It is so cold you can see your breath
when you talk,
In December I can hardly wait for
Father Christmas to visit with a
sackful of presents.

Carolyn Ward (11)
St Francis De Sales Junior School

My Top Ten Pop Groups

I like Spice Girls, they're so great.
I like Aaron Carter, he's my mate.
I like Hanson because of their hair.
I like Backstreet Boys because they're fair.
I like OTT because they're over the top.
I like All Saints, they're into pop.
I like Cleopatra for they are only a few.
I like Ant and Dec, there's only two.
I like Kavanna, he's alright.
I like Louise, she sings just right.

Serene Antony (10)
St Francis De Sales Junior School

SUMMER DAYS

On summer days
children play, dogs sleep.

On summer days
kittens are born, ice-cream flows.

On summer days
school is out, accidents happen.

On summer days
no work, people sleeping.

On summer days
sports on, tired children.

On summer days
not a minute to lose, places to go.

On summer days
clothes get bought, toys get sold.

On summer days
we go out to the beach, see good friends.

On summer days
dates to be made, girls to see.

On summer days
the heat rises, minute by minute.

On summer days
you can't stand the increasing heat.

On summer days
I sit quiet, telling my lonely tale.

On summer days
I myself am rushing place to place.

On summer days
the weather is cool, people happy people sad.

Andrew Ayim (9)
St Francis De Sales Junior School

SCHOOL

School, such a delightful place to be,
Teachers pay for their steamy appetising tea,
Children sitting in their comfy seats,
In their uniform they all look so sweet!

It came to a day class five's teacher was off,
They had a supply teacher who was tough,
That didn't stop them from being bad,
When the teacher came back she went mad.

The teacher thought and thought what to do,
Because of their bad behaviour while she had the flu,
She made them clean the headteacher's room,
The children were all filled with gloom.

The children were absolutely fed up,
So they bought their teacher a little china cup,
The teacher let them off and said 'Alright,'
'Miss next time let us off a little light.'

Rachel Adu (10)
St Francis De Sales Junior School

FRIENDS

Friends friends, lovely friends
I have lots of friends
Kind and caring
Friendly and fun
We play all the time and I make new friends, friends, friends
Laugh and giggle
Hate and love
Play with all different friends, friends
Friends
I have lots of friends,
Friends, friends, friends.

Shane Dacosta (9)
St Francis De Sales Junior School

SPRING

Eggs hatch in the spring,
then the birds begin to sing.
Sometimes there's sunshine in the day,
then it starts to go away.

In the day it's nice and good,
we have friends in the neighbourhood.
But then we have some fun outside,
but finally it rains and we go inside.

Linda Gyamfi (9)
St Francis De Sales Junior School

THE OAK TREE AND THE BUMBLE BEE

A bumble bee once landed in an oak made strong and tough,
The oak tree then aloud he said, 'I've just had enough,
I have to stand here all day long,
I don't know why I've done nothing wrong!
I want to see the world so sweet,
I want to see what people eat,
And so my dear bee,
I wish I were thee!'
The bumble bee with one loud sigh,
said quickly in reply,
'I don't know what you're talking about,
I wish to be a tree so stout,
For every time when I am seen,
I hear a shout then a scream,
Then try to harm me, oh they do,
And so you see I wish I were you!'

Natasha Socrates (9)
St Francis De Sales Junior School

COLOURS

Yellow is the warm sun.
Blue is the shivering stream.
Red is the burning flames.
White is the midnight moon.
Black is the pitch dark roads.
Green is the summer trees.
Grey is the frosty mist.
Orange is the burning sun.
Brown is the birds' nest.

Lauren Perry (10)
St Francis De Sales Junior School

DOUBLE TROUBLE

My cousin is so annoying,
She's weird in a sort of way,
She leaps up and down
and runs round and round
she gets weirder every day.
I baby-sit her sometimes
to try and secretly see,
but she locks herself in her room
and throws away the key.
I never will quite understand her
whatever could it be?
I think she's got some kind of fever,
but don't ask me!

Lucy Matthias (9)
St John Evangelist RC Primary School

FULL OF FAME!

Oh how I admire,
this thing hotter than fire,
it has a name,
this thing is full of fame.
Even by using a ladder,
you couldn't reach this thing,
it belongs to everyone
it doesn't ring or sing,
it just stays still.

Never look directly at this
thing it will blind you!

What is my riddle?

Catherine Courtney-Diggins (9)
St John Evangelist RC Primary School

MY HAMSTER MATILDA

I have a hamster
she is cute and sweet
I named her Matilda
and she likes to eat

Matilda listens to me
every word I say
She likes to eat nuts
and she likes to play

She has a soft coat
it is brown and white
she scratches at her cage
and keeps me up all night

Matilda also eats apples
and she eats sunflower seeds
and if I do not feed her
she will always plead

Matilda is my baby
but she tries to run
and if I do not play with her
she will still have fun

I have a hamster
she is small and sweet
she loves her name Matilda
and she still loves to eat.

Holly Seabrook (9)
St John Evangelist RC Primary School

EMOTIONS

When I'm walking home from school
I can't get anything off my mind
like how I dream my life away
with my head stuck up in the clouds.

I think of all those happy days
when I was a part of the crowd
but now I stand out of the crowd
like I am something strange.

Nevertheless when I walk into the park
it fills my heart with joy
to see every tree, puddle and lake
dancing happily in the breeze.

I love to play by the weeping willow tree
and sit reading in the sun
and watch the children playing merrily
this is how I like to have fun.

When it gets dark I have to depart
but all the time I'm thinking of the park
the park is an inspiration to laugh and play
instead of working in school all day.

Jane Egan (9)
St John Evangelist RC Primary School

THE THIN WOMAN

There was a very thin woman
as thin as a pin
She ate nothing from a pea
to a pin
She looked very silly
and had a son called Billy.

Billy was a young fellow
as fat as a ball,
people think he looks like you
like a twit or what are you.

Danny Saward (11)
St John Evangelist RC Primary School

THE HECTIC GRANNY!

I have a granny,
She is not at all funny,
She drives us all insane
And gives us loads of pain.

If you just know
Just what I have in store
For you!

I want a snail,
And a worm two
And a horrid monkey from the zoo.
Will she explode?
I am not so sure
Will she go bang
Or will she run down into the loo
Or maybe down the zoo?

Oh granny I am so sorry
But if you just knew

I am so glad it's not me!

I'd rather be a chimpanzee . . .

Lillina Capillo (11)
St John Evangelist RC Primary School

I HAVE A BLACK CAT

I have a black cat
He's short and fat
He sits on a mat
And acts like a bat

There he lies
In front of a fire
With his milk and tea and sugar

He lays in a ball
And plays with his ball
And he has black stone eyes
That look so terrifying

He is the worst laziest cat
I have ever known
That sits on a mat
And acts like a bat

At night he is so loud
He thinks he is so proud
He looks up at the clouds
And says he is the proudest cat ever.

Colleen Donaghey (11)
St John Evangelist RC Primary School

MARY, MARY QUITE CONTRARY WITH A TWIST

Mary, Mary
heard your garden is dead.
I heard a bomb came down last night,
and exploded in the flower bed.

Did any of your precious flowers survive,
are any of them still alive?
Were all of them blown to bits,
the bomber really got a good hit.

I'm sorry about your garden, dear,
it's such an awful shame,
but all your flowers will grow back soon,
all the same.

Now I come to the end of my letter,
because I've things to do,
but then you'll never be able to read it
'cause you got blown to bits too.

Roisin Healy (11)
St John Evangelist RC Primary School

GRANDMA

My gran is like an armchair, nice
and welcome. She is like a cuddly bear.
She is black like the night.
And she is soft like a teddy.
She is juicy like a sweet pear.
She is yellow like hot sun.

Jefferson Anyanwu (9)
St John Evangelist RC Primary School

THE GOLDEN SUNFLOWER

I lay on my couch and think,
what a wonderful day it's been
with the sparkling sunflowers and
the darkest grass I have ever seen.
With the sounds from downstream
the sunflower gleam
but the happy song so powerful
the sadness faded away
and the happinesss brought back spring.
As I walked home
all alone I still thought I was with
the sparkling sunflowers
that made the grass blossom.

Toni Mia Corbyn (9)
St John Evangelist RC Primary School

MY BIRD THE CAT AND THE DOG

I have a bird,
He is blue
And is a nerd
And eats a lot too

He was chased by a cat
Who was chased by a dog
Whose owner was fat
They ran past a boy who was playing with a Pog

The dog bashed the cat
The owner
Who was very fat
Bashed the dog

The cat got away
He had a toy
And went to play
With the boy.

Christopher Owens (11)
St John Evangelist RC Primary School

GEORGE

I have a pet
Oh he's such a pest
He's not cute,
But to me he's the best

He swings on the curtains
He rocks the baby
His name is George
And he can say 'Maybe.'

He barks at the door
And dances to a song,
He loves a walk and
Visiting the pond.

When he died
I screamed and shouted
Most of all tears I cried.

Toni Young (11)
St John Evangelist RC Primary School

MARMALADE AND POG!

I have a cat called Marmalade
and a dog called Pog
Marmalade drinks cherryade
and Pog eats chocolate log.

During the night
they both always fight
and never get along
they keep me up all night by going
bing, bing, bing and bong, bong, bong.

So one night I got a gun
and shot a bun at them
they ate all the bun
and then began to have some fun.

But at the end I like them both
and they like each other too
it's just as much I hope you know
it's me who likes you too.

Natalie Walsh (11)
St John Evangelist RC Primary School

MY CAT HENRY

I have a cat called Henry,
He is pretty fat,
He walks into the door,
And never uses the mat.

He plays with the furniture,
He rolls across the floor,
He comes in the cat flap,
Underneath the door.

When my cat starts to eat,
He always ends up with smelly feet,
I really should stop feeding him,
He gets too fat and is rather dim.

One day, I sadly say,
My cat Henry has passed away,
I want to get a new cat,
That is rather not so very fat.

Kelly Hughes (10)
St John Evangelist RC Primary School

PETS

I have a dog
Who's just the best!
I have a cat
Who's such a pest.

I have a bird
Who's such a nerd
I have a mole
Who lives in a hole.

I have a monkey
Who eats all my mum's pans
He jumps on the furniture
And acts like Tarzan.

Maa-Abena Owusu-Kyereko (11)
St John Evangelist RC Primary School

MY CAT MONKEY

My cat Monkey
Is so hunky
He looks so chunky
But he is funky.

He sits on my lap every day
I love him so much
That I hope he won't die,
But still I think he will
Go one day and I don't know why.

One day he died
And yes I cried
I was very sad
But just having a cat like
Monkey made me really glad.

Penny Wilkins (11)
St John Evangelist RC Primary School

MY FISH BILLY

I have a fish called Billy
I see him every day
I always have to feed him
Every single day

I always eat my fish
Because I like them too
Whenever I run out of fish
I cook Billy in a stew

You might think it's cruel
But when I ran out of fish
I can't live without them
So I put Billy in a dish

After two minutes
You will see nothing in the plate
I am a fish fan
But not Billy's mate.

Charles Oluwashola Adefeye (10)
St John Evangelist RC Primary School

I HAVE A RAT

I have a rat
His name is Pat
But he is so fat
That's why I named him Pat.

He loves to play
After he lays
In his hay
And sleeps all day

He loves his mate
His name is Tate
He plays with plates
He's always late

He likes cats
He wants to sit on the mat
Because his mate ate
And is like a fire.

Stevie Larkins (11)
St John Evangelist RC Primary School

THE EXPERTS!

Give three cheers for experts,
They know a thing or two,
And if we didn't have them,
Whatever would we do?

They built a ship that never sank,
It sailed across the sea,
The name was Titanic,
It's gone down in history.

For years and years the experts knew,
That the sun went round the earth,
Then one scientist said 'Wrong'
The earth goes round the sun.

Natalie Cameron (10)
St John Evangelist RC Primary School

A BON OF BONFIRE NIGHT

You hear the bang
On bonfire night
Everybody enjoying themselves
With sparklers and rockets
Lots of sweets in their pockets
Bang! Boom! Wheee! Bash
That's what you hear on bonfire night
Everybody going out
Spending their money on rockets
Lighting them late at night
The rockets are as bright as a star
And as colourful as a waterfall.

Alix Balding (10)
St John Evangelist RC Primary School

I HAVE A BIRD

I have a bird called Jesse,
he is very messy.
He has a sister called Bessy,
who flies very fast.

The problem with Bessy,
is she is more messy
and that's why I don't like Bessy
who flies very fast.

'Oh please!' said Bessy
'I know I'm messy,'
'But please' said Bessy
'Let me stay a night.'

'OK,' said Jesse
'But you're so messy,'
'I know' said Bessy,
'But there's nothing I can do.

The next night Jesse and Bessy
had been so messy,
that Jesse and Bessy
blamed each other.

'Oh! Go away Bessy
You're just too messy'
'OK,' said Bessy
'I'm going now!'

Tara Santiago (11)
St John Evangelist RC Primary School

MUD

Mud mud
everywhere
in my shoes
and in my hair
when I make it
go away
it comes back
and's there to stay.

It always comes
after me
I'm a good boy
can't they see,
by the way
my name is Scot
the thing is I cry a lot.

I always try getting it off
you need more than
a cloth
I pull and yank to
see it go
but it's too fast and
I'm too slow.

It finally went
far away
but there's something
I sadly say
It went on my
best friend Vince
and I've never
ever seen him since.

Danny Roberts (11)
St John Evangelist RC Primary School

MY BIRDS

I have a bird
He is a nerd
He is absurd
And likes to be heard

I went to the shop
I heard a shot
My mum was very hot
And my bird was tied up and shot

I went to the pet shop to buy a bird
Who's not a nerd
And definitely not absurd
And it was the third bird I had

His name is Billy
He is very silly
He lives up a tree
And drinks cold tea

He went on the road
And got eaten by a toad
And that was the end of silly Bill
For ever.

Seamus Quinn (10)
St John Evangelist RC Primary School

SNAKE

One day I found a snake
and it was sucking my drink.
It slithered along, making a trail.
It looked beautiful and
as straight as a rake.

It licked its lips
as it slid along through the grass.
It was bright green and
its tongue was red.
Its back was scaly and it had
flaps of skin on its cheeks.

It held its neck up high,
its beady eyes glinting in the sun.
Then it seemed to see something
and headed towards the trees.
It raised its head, suddenly
it struck at a large beetle.

Imogen Louise Thompson (7)
St John's Highbury Vale School

WHAT WOULD HAPPEN IF I . . .?

What would happen if I put jam on my dad's favourite suit?
What would happen if I stuck a cream cracker in the computer?
What would happen if I cut off my sister's hair?
What would happen if I ate the clay pot my mum made?
What would happen if I tore up my grandad's passport?
What would happen if I smashed my brother's violin?
Maybe I will try these things tomorrow!

Ned Kelly (8)
St John's Highbury Vale School

MY HAMSTER IS TINY MAGIC

My hamster is Tiny Magic.
It runs around and scurries up mouse holes,
pipes and arms and sleeves.
It tickles your finger if you're one it knows
and if it doesn't it will bite off your nose.

My hamster is Tiny Magic.
In the day it's fast asleep in
pink and yellow fluffy fluff.
At night it opens its eyes to do its exercise.

My hamster is Tiny Magic.
It likes its nutty hamster treats
nuts, fruit and vegetables.
It nibbles away all night
it is such a sight.

Francesca Hughes-Campbell (7)
St John's Highbury Vale School

ONE OF THE PLACES I LIKE BEST

One of the places I like best
is the cool, calm, ice-skating rink.
When I am skating on that wonderful place,
from here to there in a wink.

Skating along in a funny way
I twist and turn in a frenzy,
Cool! I've just done a twist . . . *Hooray!*
I wave to Mrs McKenzie.

Naomi Ellen Speechley (8)
St John's Highbury Vale School

JUNGLE ANIMALS

Jungle animals wash and play,
In their jungle home all day.
Muddy feet will make a track,
To the watering hole and back.

With crinkly skin and shooting spout,
The elephant roams and slops about.
He moves slowly, but is not in danger,
No one he sees is ever a stranger.

At the top of the forest tall,
The parrots and budgies squawk and call.
The colours are bright: red, yellow and green,
A flash of bright colour can be suddenly seen.

Sleeping under a shady rock,
The jungle lizard gets a shock.
When passing through his leafy home,
The spotty leopard comes to roam.

The slithery snake goes through the grass,
He lets most animals wander past.
But if someone prances on the snake,
They will be poisoned, no mistake.

Funny monkey on a rail,
Swinging downwards with his tail.
As he swings from tree to tree,
I want to be like him, so free.

Endangered species, flowers and trees,
Things that fly around like bees.
Fierce or shy, all are alive,
But now need our help just to survive.

Joanna Faulkner (7)
St John's Highbury Vale School

THE LOON RACE

Out on the moon
There was a baboon
The baboon's name was Loon
And then one morning in outer space
The baboon found an awkward place
He found a funny face
And then they raced
Loon was the ace
But the face . . .
Just then the baboon's Aunt Grace
Came into the great big space
'Give me my Loon!'
And that was the end of the Loon race.

Lindsay Beck (7)
St John's Highbury Vale School

MY BUDGIE

I have a budgie named Sky
She is white and blue
She spreads her wings oh so high
She is very cute too.

She likes to play around
And bite me with her beak
She hardly makes a sound
We always play hide and seek.

She loves her food called Honey Bell
She's one thing I'll never sell
She is always kneeling on my dad
And my dad replies you're very bad.

Zahra Franklin (10)
St Joseph's RC Primary School

HOMEWORK

Go away homework, I hate you, you stink,
I wish I could crush you or pour you down the sink.

Homework, I'm fed up, won't you go away,
You better be gone by the end of the day.

Go away homework, you're going to cause a storm,
But don't do it now 'cause I'm trying to keep warm.

Go away homework, it's 12 o'clock noon,
There's a few hours left so you better go soon.

Go away homework, I'm having my dinner,
You can't stop me eating or else I'll get thinner.

Okay then homework, I give up, you win,
But it won't be over until you're in the bin.

or

Okay then homework, I give up, you win,
But it isn't over till the fat lady sings.

Thomas Chigbo (10)
St Joseph's RC Primary School

IRON CHAOS

The iron man is fierce,
The iron man is scary,
The iron man is always hungry
And he's coming right towards me!

I feel the ground shaking,
I think I'm going to scream,
The iron man is coming,
His shiny iron gleams.

I'm running as fast as I can,
I'm screaming, 'Help, help, help!'
I don't think anyone is coming,
But the iron man is!

Good, I'm near my house,
I don't think I can run anymore,
I see my mum open the door,
Let me in and bang the door!

Colette Tunney (9)
St Joseph's RC Primary School

SCHOOL HISTORY

I like teachers
they have nice features
every day,
in every way.

I love my reading books
it doesn't matter about their pictures,
looks
we're outside playing with the ball
when grown-ups call us in the hall.

We were in the hall, ready to sing
when we heard the bell ring
the teacher said 'Out, but don't you
dare shout.'
The fire bells were ringing
no time for the singing
until the bells stop ringing.

Ria Ioannou (8)
St Joseph's RC Primary School

IRON MAN BEWARE

The iron man is a
big old fellow with feet as
big as single beds and a body
taller than a house.
Stomp, stomp, stomp.

With eyes that change
colour, from blue to white,
and thumbs that are as big as
human hands.
Stomp, stomp, stomp.

You better watch out,
before you get crushed
by those giant toes and feet.
Stomp, stomp, stomp.

Aha go quick we're going
to get tramped.
Hurry, hurry up, oh phew
he's gone.
Thank goodness for that.
Stomp, stomp, stomp.

Emma Nolan (9)
St Joseph's RC Primary School

THE WIND

The wind, the wind rushing breeze,
Shaking the trees, bending the leaves.
Hear the howling, hear the noises,
Blowing cans and blowing the dust,
Higher and higher as the wind blows,
Over the buildings, over the sea.

When the wind begins to fade,
Everything has changed.
All the leaves are on the ground,
Nothing makes a sound.
Everything has gone away,
But the wind might come the next day.

Kaho Cheung (10)
St Joseph's RC Primary School

WINTER WONDERLAND

In the winter wonderland,
Crystal snowflakes fall,
A blanket of fluffy white,
And snowmen straight and tall.

It's very cold and nippy outside,
I'm wearing my scarf and gloves,
But the snow lying on the ground,
Is like one thousand doves.

I pad along through the snow,
The icicles fall around,
And as the snow softly falls,
It doesn't make a sound.

Every tree is out of sight,
Hidden beneath the snow,
Usually the birds are singing now,
But I can't find a crow.

I look inside my window,
The snow swirls calmly down,
And little heaps are formed,
And a snowflake is like a crown.

Rachel Kenny (10)
St Joseph's RC Primary School

THE IRON MAN IS BACK

The iron man walks,
while he talks,
stamping through the forest.
Here he goes and throws
the big rock, so watch out.
'Bang! Bang! Bang!

The iron man is grey metal,
when he is boiling like
a kettle.
The iron man goes
where nobody knows.
Bang! Bang! Bang!

The iron man
is big like a giant,
his leg is big,
as big as his bed.
Bang! Bang! Bang!

The iron man goes
to the cliff,
but doesn't know where
it is, crash, bash,
gone for a splash,
Bang! Bang! Bang!

Caius Dolan (9)
St Joseph's RC Primary School

THE IRON MAN IN TROUBLE

The iron man is big,
the iron man is strong,
bigger, bigger, bigger than
a kite.
His eyes are mean and green.
He likes cars and bars to eat.

His body is grey and shiny.
People are scared of him
as he is big and strong.
He wrecks the farmer's shed,
the farmer's in trouble.
The country hate the iron man
and so the iron man wrecks
the farm again.

Nathan De Souza (8)
St Joseph's RC Primary School

THE WIND

Wind, wind hear it go
Shaking! Rattling! Roaring!
Swirling, whirling over the seas
Crashing, dashing through the air
Twisting, whistling in the trees
Getting faster
Gushing, rushing wherever it goes
Now it's dying gently away
Sweetly swaying side to side
Just a sweet, soft breeze
Gone, ready to come another day.

Annette Shiel (10)
St Joseph's RC Primary School

SCHOOL HISTORY

My school is very, very old,
At least it is not cold.
Sometimes work is hard,
Teachers, not that bad.

Pencils, pens and writing books,
I don't care about their looks.
If the pencils are blue, if the pencils are black,
I won't need to give them back.

Reading books,
And coat hooks.
Playtime is fun,
But it would be good, if we could lie in the sun.

Sonia Fullerton (9)
St Joseph's RC Primary School

ON MY WAY TO SCHOOL

On my way to school Miss,
I know you won't believe this,
I was beamed up by aliens Miss,
and taken into space Miss.
They put a probe up my nose Miss,
to examine my brain Miss,
much to their surprise Miss,
nothing was found Miss,
much to their disgust Miss.
They sent me back to earth Miss,
that's why I was late Miss,
but just in time for lunch Miss!

Veronica Castro (11)
St Joseph's RC Primary School

THE IRON MAN STRIKES

The iron man is very grumpy,
The iron man is very lumpy,
The iron man is very crusty,
The iron man is very rusty.

The iron man eats metal,
he likes to eat some iron petals,
climbing up the cliff,
falling crash, boom, crack, whoops,
lying silent on the beach, up he gets on his feet.

Trying to get him back together,
flying around like a flying feather,
click, click, goes his eyes,
we always say 'We're going to fly.'

Why did he come? Nobody knows,
Why is he here? Nobody knows,
everyone knows what to do, run!
Stomp, stomp, stomp, where is he gone.

Yes he has gone, wow!
Let's put on some song,
dancing and talking,
flying and pouncing,
Stomp, stomp, stomp, what's that.

Leanna Seewoochurn (9)
St Joseph's RC Primary School

MASTER OF THE METAL FACTORY

Master of the
metal factory
always walking
around, tasting things
he should not
touch and always
looking down.

Master of the
metal factory
is getting really
sad and people
are treating
him really bad.

Master of the
metal factory
looking into
homes, but
sometimes he
always finds
a little telephone.

Master of the
metal factory
going to the city
dump looking
around for food
thump, thump,
thump.

Makhala Boyd-Little (9)
St Joseph's RC Primary School

SMOKING AND DRINKING

I was walking down the alleyway,
I see someone smoking,
The person who was smoking thought I was joking,
When I told him he was gonna die,
He thought I was telling *a big, fat lie.*

Smoking and drinking is very bad,
Smoking and drinking don't make you glad,
It makes your lungs go black and blue
And that's why it's not good for you.

I was walking down the alleyway,
Someone with an alcoholic drink,
It made him go
Purple and pink.

Smoking and drinking is very bad,
Smoking and drinking don't make you glad,
It makes your lungs go back and blue,
That's why it's not good for *you!*

Matthew Mattioli (11)
St Joseph's RC Primary School

BIG TALL IRON MAN

Big, tall iron man walking down the street
cars are beeping right at your feet.
Run, run iron man, the Army's on your tail
run, run iron man or you will be in jail.

Iron man, iron man the time has arrived
run, run quick, go and hide.
Iron man, iron man it's dinner time
you're supposed to go to the restaurant
with Hanot Hide.

Iron man, iron man people are here
and they are throwing very big spheres.
Run, run or they will hunt you like a deer.
Iron man, iron man you are free
if you go over that mountain to your Aunt Bean.

Oliver Beccles (9)
St Joseph's RC Primary School

SCHOOL

School is uncool,
Children be quiet or you will
cause a riot.
How I hate teachers, I'd rather go to lovely
beaches than be with those teachers.

Some children rock on their
chairs and some children jump up the
stairs but they all hate *school*
but I suppose I have to learn.

I learn how to read
and how to plant a seed
but I still
hate school.

Maxine Reynolds (8)
St Joseph's RC Primary School

PEACE

Peace is out, peace is about, peace is everywhere.

Torturing fights
leaves peace alight
in burning flames.

With broken hearts
like dagger darts
and people short of peace
between them and their
neighbours.

Pieces of shattered glass
and damaged hearts
left in the darkness.

No harmony.

Kylie Marie McManus (11)
St Joseph's RC Primary School

THE WIND

Feel the wind gushing through the trees
with a very cool breeze.
Whirling and swirling over the houses
leaving bits of rubbish scattered in all directions,
as it moves on.
Whistling and churning,
getting faster and faster,
banging and rattling
as it hits every window.
Gushing forth to see what next
picking up speed
every minute,
as the trees sway to and fro
rattling its leaves as the wind goes away.
As the wind goes on it gradually gets slow,
with a soft whisper
the wind dies away.

Chika Obi (9)
St Joseph's RC Primary School

STORM

I wake up to hear the bashing
and clashing of the storm,
to watch the menacing lightning
like a knife cutting through the sky.
The wind so strong it pulls down trees.
A fork of lightning comes down just
missing a tree.
Slates are tumbling off the roof and
come crashing down,
followed by a crash through my window
as the old tree falls through my window
into my room.
Boom, the thunder has struck again
like cymbals clashing together,
leaves fly up towards the light
of flashing lightning,
the last clash of thunder and
the storm has died out,
it's moved on,
with it the thunder and lightning
trailing behind.

Stephanie Tonge (10)
St Joseph's RC Primary School

MY DOG BEN

My dog Ben
has cute puppy eyes.
His smooth coat
pants when he lies.

My dog Ben
never ever bites
but growls when we switch off the lights.

My dog Ben
has a big green ball
he loves it so
he runs for it when I call.

My dog Ben
is a passionate dog.
He jumps on your head for one single kiss.

Lisa Marie Spikesley (10)
St Joseph's RC Primary School

THE GREAT STORM

Great booming of thunder and crashing of lightning,
Rustling of bushes and trees,
A strong gush of wind which knocked down a tree,
Trees swaying to and fro,
Stormy weather at this time is dashing through the woods,
The rain is coming and people start to put up hoods.

Orange coloured leaves gushing through the breeze,
Rattling, swirling, whirling and it's howling like a wolf,
Mad zig-zagedy lightning like a knife,
The doors of houses are knocked in,
Rage of roaring coming from the sky.

Avalanches in polar climates are knocking houses down,
Huge snowballs and icicles are killing people too.
The raging sea is crashing against the sea dock,
The time is up for the wind,
It has travelled a long way.

Ailish Mooney (9)
St Joseph's RC Primary School

THE DOLPHIN SHOW

I watch the dolphins jump up into
the clear blue sky.
They jump up one by one
as if they want to go
over the clouds.
Then a little girl comes up
to give the three dolphins
a fish each.
The girl tosses three fishes
into the air
and all three dolphins catch
the fish with a great big splash.
Later on in the show
it is time for the dolphins to go to sleep
to have their little nap.

Chemaine Constant (10)
St Joseph's RC Primary School

MY FAMILY

Sometimes my mother is happy,
Sometimes my mother is sad,
Sometimes my mother can be angry,
Sometimes my mother can be calm.
But I will always love her.

Sometimes my father is funny,
Sometimes my father is boring,
Sometimes my father can be very angry,
Sometimes my father can be very calm,
But I will always love him.

Sometimes my brother is sharing,
Sometimes my brother is daring,
Sometimes my brother can be good,
sometimes my brother can be bad,
But I will always love him.

Zerlinda Ranasinghe (10)
St Joseph's RC Primary School

THE HAUNTED HOUSE

When you walk past the haunted house,
You'd better be as quiet as a mouse.
Because you might get caught by the ghoul
And the bats might make you fall.

When you walk past the haunted garden,
If you burp you'd better say pardon.
If you don't you'll be in a mess
And the ghosts will put you in a dress.

When you walk through the haunted graveyard
I wouldn't complain that it looks like lard.
Guess who lives there? The vampire.
He'll bite your neck till it burns like fire.

If you get past the haunted house test,
You just have to deal with one more pest.
He calls himself the Great Gatekeeper.
To get home you'll have to be a great leaper.

Come, come it's fun to be one,
They will give you a free bun.
If you come you can sit by me,
It's good being the nice 'keeper.

Matthew Callinan (10)
St Joseph's RC Primary School

WINTERTIME

People skating on the winter ice,
children are playing,
the fog comes closer,
as the snow trickles down.

The snow becomes icicles,
upon the window-ledges,
you can smell stew,
cooking in the houses.

Cars coming down the snowy roads,
people slipping as they walk,
the fog's still getting closer,
the cars are going slower.

The stew is ready,
everyone's at home,
the clock strikes nine,
time for bed.

People snoring in the cold winter's night,
children are sleeping,
not letting the bed bugs bite,
and that's all till springtime.

Sophie Watson (10)
St Joseph's RC Primary School

A WINTER POEM

The clock strikes six
in a still, wintry village,
whilst the mist rises
upon the frost covered hills.

Children playing on their sledges,
racing down the slope;
till the snow awakes
and trickles down.

Look out of the window
to see the pretty snowflakes
sitting on the window-ledge,
and then the pretty sight melts to the ground.

Animals are now hibernating,
robins are nesting on evergreen trees;
children are eating hot food and drink
but don't forget it's Christmas Eve.

The clock strikes seven
in the still, wintry village,
the sky gets dark
covering the land.

Iria Lopez (10)
St Joseph's RC Primary School

THE HURRICANE

It's a cloudy day,
Everybody hates it,
It's starting to rain,
Everybody hates it,
It's raining harder,
Everybody hates it,
Harder and harder,
Everybody hates it,
Boom, boom, boom!
Bang, bang, bang!
Sh, sh, sh, sh!
The storm is coming,
The rain is very hard,
The storm is here,
Everybody hates it,
They're screaming and screaming,
Everybody hates it,
'Help! Help!' the children cry,
Everybody hates it,
The hurricane is here,
It blows the roofs off,
It gets the cars that are parked on the road,
It gets some people,
The hurricane is gone,
Everybody loves it.

Pablo Castro (9)
St Joseph's RC Primary School

NIGHTMARE

I rest my head, my eyelids close,
I fall asleep, I start to doze.
The thunder cracks inside my head,
I twist and turn upon my bed.
I imagine hungry, menacing creatures,
With piercing eyes and terrible features.
I close my eyes, I start to scream,
I'm a prisoner in my dream.
The thunder cracks, the creatures flee,
I run and hide behind a tree.
An eerie sound echoes through the wood,
I try to run, but it's no good.
Fire breaks out and spreads around,
The creatures howl in the background.
I wake with a sigh of relief,
But it is my firm belief
That the dark recesses of the brain,
Often bring joy, but always more pain.

Daniel Roberts (10)
St Joseph's RC Primary School

SNOW

Snow is like a white brick wall
built along
the dry summer's
closing door,
all the winter hats
look like little peas
spread along the
white brick wall.

Andrew Frank Judge (11)
St Joseph's RC Primary School

CARIBBEAN POEM

Jamaica is famous,
Jamaica is good.
Jamaica is hot
so come along.

Eat some bulla,
Eat some pone.
Eat some lovely food,
some come along.

Jamaica is famous,
Jamaica is good.
Jamaica is hot
so come here too.

Boys playing football,
so can oono
the sun is hot
very, very hot.

Jamaica is famous,
Jamaica is good.
Jamaica is hot
so come along!

Mangoes
and ripe bananas,
jelly coconut
and pomegranates.

Jamaica is famous,
Jamaica is good.
Jamaica is hot
so . . .
come here now!

Dean Da Conceicao (10)
St Joseph's RC Primary School

IRONBRIDGE

On a very fine day,
we were on our way,
to visit the Ironbridge.

The sun shone bright,
at the beautiful sight,
of the famous three-arched bridge.

High up on the bridge,
I could see the ridge,
of the river below.

The River Severn's seaweed-green colour,
the likes of which I have never seen before.
Flowed right beneath us, like a carpet on the floor.

As the sun set in the east,
back to the hostel for a feast
without delay and discuss our day.
Hip, hip, hooray.

Kieran Dixon-Smith (11)
St Joseph's RC Primary School

LOVE

Every time I look in his eyes
my heart jumps.
I will give my life for him.
Before I met him
I was in total darkness.
When I met him
my life lit up.

Musu Kapu (11)
St Joseph's RC Primary School

PEACE SHOULD BE AROUND US

P is for peace around the world
E is for endrance to the nation
A is for allowing people to love them
C is for a Catholic who loves
E is for energy to work for the poor.

They don't ask for much
All they want is a little help and love.
Jesus died on the cross to save us from evil.
Nobody would ever do that for you nor me.
And maybe some day there will be peace
everywhere.
I pray.

Victoria Kotun (11)
St Ignatius RC Primary School

PEACE

P is for peace and no war,
E is for energy,
A is for asleep,
C is for citizen,
E is for effectuate.

There is not peace everywhere in
the world, but maybe one day there
will be peace everywhere.

Let there be peace in the world.

Zehra Suleyman (10)
St Ignatius RC Primary School

PEACE

We all need peace
No war, more peace
You fight and you fight
You wish you had peace
But you don't know how
You try and you try
But people won't listen
Then you die now.

People hear of the grief
And they start to cry
They wish they had peace
They don't know why
They try to stop fighting
But people want to win
They start to beg for peace
People still won't listen
And they die of grief.

Houses get torn down
More people start to cry
They pray to their God, to stop this war.
Families and friends
Try to run
They can't escape, for fear or peace
They can't escape the dreadful game.

Fighting turns into peace
People start to agree
They follow the rules
Of peace and harmony
So stay in peace, all countries of the world
And you will be safe from all wicked works.

Mojisola Awojobi (10)
St Ignatius RC Primary School

PEACE

Silent quiet and unknown
What do you think?

Creeping on your own
What do you think?

Peace is a symbol
You should know
What do you think?

Give me reason I should know.
What do you think?

My mother said peacefully
'It's time for bed'
What do you think?

Tamara Bello (11)
St Ignatius RC Primary School

PEACE

Peace, peace is all we need, save us from a lot of grief.
Peace, peace is all we need, shake a hand and that is peace.
Peace, peace is all we need, save the planet make some peace.
Peace, peace is all we need, bring some different people
together and there you are you'll have some peace.
So come on and let's make peace from every nation,
let's make peace whatever the colour, whatever the nation.

Ray Ansah Adjapong (11)
St Ignatius RC Primary School

WHERE IS PEACE?

When guns shoot out and
People die, what a terrible
Place for peace, when farmers,
Crops are destroyed, what a
Terrible place for peace,
And people die of hunger
What terrible place for
Peace, when noises are
Everywhere and you can't
Go to sleep, what a terrible
Place for peace, when young
Kids die or they're split from
Their families, what a terrible
Place for peace, when your class
And teacher are shot to death
What a terrible place for peace,
Place with war and people
Die, Sri Lanka, Sri Lanka,
Peace be with you.

Evalyn Wambulu (10)
St Ignatius RC Primary School

MAKE PEACE TODAY

We would all like peace in our day,
That is all we would pray,
To love each other we would all say,
We want peace every day,
To not kill anybody, anyway,
So let's say peace every day.

Ashley Joseph (11)
St Ignatius RC Primary School

WHY PEACE?

Why does love turn to hate whenever things go wrong?
Why do people hurt each other
and cause each other pain?
Oh, I wish we could start again.

Just think of a world with no more pain
A world with lots of smiles
Where laughter and love was everywhere
Oh, I wish we could start again.

My name is Joanne, I'm 11 years old
But my future feels so sad
Because they're hating, hurting and killing each other.
Tell me, has the whole world gone mad?

The world is a wonderful place to be
If only they'd open their eyes and see
That beauty and peace could be everywhere
Yes, a wonderful world it could be.

Joanne Britto (11)
St Ignatius RC Primary School

PEACE IN THE WORLD

Make peace not war,
Or the outcome will be sore,
Make the world a better place,
Let the world show its grace,
Don't make it worse,
Or you'll have lots to nurse
So make peace,
Let war cease.

Reag Bermejo (11)
St Ignatius RC Primary School

PEACE IS WHAT WE NEED

What do we need?
Peace!
Say it again.
Peace!
Peace, peace is a good thing and that's what we all need.
So don't start a war, that's not what we all need.
Bring war countries peace.
We should be making everyone happy.
Let's heal the world with love and care.
So what do we need?
Peace!
Say it again.
Peace!
Thank you for making the world a better place.

Seona Scott (11)
St Ignatius RC Primary School

PEACE

Let there be peace shared among us
Let there be peace in our heart
May now peace sweet this nation cause
us oh Lord to arise,
Give us a fresh understanding
Brotherly peace that is real
May now your peace be together.
     May now
     your
     peace.

Seymona Cole (11)
St Ignatius RC Primary School

WARS AND PEACE

Let there be peace
everywhere we go,
there shouldn't be violence anywhere.
There should be no wars around
other people or us.
Everyone should be happy, nice and caring
about those people who have wars around
them and should support them.
There shouldn't be wars between states
and countries.
There should be no fighting between any
countries, states, villages, cities and towns.
Everyone should be a peace maker
and there should be friends from one
country to another one.

Joanne Adamu (11)
St Ignatius RC Primary School

PEACE

Let *peace* be united
Let *people* shake hands
Let America shake hands of Iraq or Iran
Let *peace* be united with America or Iraq
Let *peace* be united with the Tamils and the Sinhales
Let the people of Sri Lanka sort out their differences
Let people be united in parts of Africa
Let people shake hands in parts of Africa
Let *peace* be united
Let people shake hands.

Natasha Morton (11)
St Ignatius RC Primary School

ADRIAN MCDUFF - THE BATTLE

I hear the trumpets
The banging of the drummer boy
We shout our war cry
Arrows are launched into the air
The clashing of swords
I hear a scream
A man falls dead

I charge at the enemy with a chain and ball
I had killed a dozen of the enemy
Our kilts filled with rage, we charged on
Then I saw our hero, Macbeth
He decapitated a man's head

I plunged my mace into a man's head
An arrow just missed me
We were losing, though
Macbeth killed like a giant
As I come to my family I will remember my battle.

Obi Eze (10)
St Ignatius RC Primary School

PEACE

Peace is when we do not fight
Peace is when we don't put end to light
Peace is when we take care of each other
Peace is when we love each other
Peace is when we are not at war
Peace is when we are calm
Peace is when your life is good.

James O'Toole (11)
St Ignatius RC Primary School

THE PEACE POEM

Peace is not found in the east,
Some people there are like beasts.
Peace does not mean violence, but when
there are bombs about you must be silent.
If you don't have peace that is very, very bad,
and you might end up feeling really, really sad.
Peace is a really good thing.
It makes you happy and it makes you sing.
So always make peace and you surely
won't end up being a beast.

So make

peace!

Selly Willems (11)
St Ignatius RC Primary School

FUNNY PEOPLE

Little Harry Hooter had a very long nose,
One day it got caught in a garden hose.
His naughty little sister soon on the scene,
Turned on the water tap without being seen.
Harry's nose soon shot out,
By way of water with a mighty spout.
His sister Denise Rapp,
Although quite a nice chap,
Drove everyone mad with her constant rap,
With her wicked and cool she broke every rule.
But now she must rap through a gap
(because her brother punched her tooth out).

Justin Hayde-West (10)
St Ignatius RC Primary School

PEACE

Peace, the opposite of war.
Every person in the world wants peace.
Every day war is everywhere and in the countries
like Sri Lanka, Bosnia and many other countries.
It's like war goes on and never stops.
Eventually war stops, a good sign.
I don't know why war starts.

You see pictures and hear about the people who
lose their family and homes.
They die starving.
They have no food, only a little.
Nowhere to live, they're homeless.

A lot of fund-raising is done to raise money
but that doesn't stop the war,
so what does?

Fighting, hurting, bombing and killing
is part of war.

Friendship, kindness and sharing,
is part of peace.

Obey the peace rules!

Natalia Ramalho (11)
St Ignatius RC Primary School

THE BATTLE HAS JUST BEGAN

As I Macbeth get ready for battle,
The battle we call the deadly war,
As we sharpen our daggers and carve our shields,
I and my best friend Banquo walk side by side.
Finally we've reached (the battlefield..??)and I see men - men
standing with their shield in one hand and their daggers in the other.
Women crying with pain and sadness.
We prepare ourselves, as the battle begins.
I throw out my dagger as it fiercely shoots right in the middle
of someone's heart.
They immediately fall to the ground.
I move back and show my shield as someone throws their
dagger towards my neck.
I then lunge forward and with a strike of my dagger I chop
off their neck.
The battle has just began as I and Banquo fight side by side.

Shatall Cooke (10)
St Ignatius RC Primary School

PEACE

We should be at peace
    so we can play together
We should be at peace
    so we can get along with each other
We should be at peace
    and try not to fight
So all our countries will be all right.

Emmanuel Ukposidolo (11)
St Ignatius RC Primary School

THE SCOTS

Children screaming, screaming for their lives,
while the soldiers come in to take their right,
leaving whatever they can hunt down on.
Parents dying, soldiers bleeding, where does it end?
Terror has come and all is done, nothing to change now.
The clouds spread out like gasses in the air.
The king is dead, now who shall be our king?
Who shall we fight?
From the devil, the army left cowardly
making all the innocents silent.
One little girl crept with the soldiers saying
'When will I die.'

Funmilola Fadeyi (10)
St Ignatius RC Primary School

PEACE

How do we get along?
How do we get through the day?
How do we say 'Hello'
and pray

For Jesus is up above
blessing people who give
their love,
and helping those in pain,
when they have nothing
to gain.

Aliea Griffith (10)
St Ignatius RC Primary School

WAR!

Departing from this bloody battle for I had a bleeding
wound which had caused me to leave.
I had fought well with the English.
Pulling out my sword, I lunged at one of them.
Clish!
Clash!
The fight was long and hard.
He sliced a cut in my arm,
That made me mad.
I lashed out.
I swung my sword around my head, chopping off his.
My arm was very painful.
I looked around.
My men were doing fine.
I walked off.

Rodney Henderson (10)
St Ignatius RC Primary School

WE NEED PEACE

We need peace, peace is love.
Peace is joy, peace is all we need.
Peace is where there's no fighting.
Peace is where there's no crime.
Peace is all we need.
Peace, peace a wonderful thing.
Some people try to make peace
and some people don't but
there's one thing we really need
and that's *peace.*

Corine Lutchman (11)
St Ignatius RC Primary School

THE BATTLE

The battle was fierce and bloodthirsty,
The king's men, bravely fought face to face.
Never have I seen such a bloody and vicious battle,
Everyone's face was filled with sorrow and fear.
All but one,
Macbeth.
He proudly stands with sword in one hand and a shield in the other.
Slashing and stabbing his enemies that dare challenge him,
Though one might think that battle is terrible,
Macbeth is proud to fight for one's king.
Those who dare challenge him, fail to have glory and triumph.
For they're not as strong as Macbeth was once thought to be.
I myself hated the battle, with the splashing of guts and the rolling
of heads.
I hope no man has to fight in a battle again.

Scott Cullen (10)
St Ignatius RC Primary School

THE MIGHTY SWORD

The mighty sword was lifted into the dark
sky and was plunged into the enemy's heart.
Macbeth turned round face to face with a very big juggernaut.
The big drum was stained and the blood of men was everywhere.
Swords up in the air and dead bodies scattered here and there.
Macbeth face to face with the juggernaut.
He lifted up his sword and hit the juggernaut on his head.
Macbeth the brave!

Daniel Aderotimi (10)
St Ignatius RC Primary School

THE WARM BLOOD

It was the day of the war and there was lots of shouting and screaming.
Already to go into battle.
The drum is banging and I, Macbeth, had my sword in one hand and
my shield in the other.
We all walked forward and swords are going ten to the dozen.
Clang, clang, they went.
Noises of people dying and blood going everywhere.
The day was blue and the clouds were white.
There was more than 20 men.
But I, Macbeth, the warrior know I can defeat them.
So the bodies are laying there dead.
The bodies are starting to rot.
The people's eyes are blurred and bones are there.

Nicholas Dorsett (10)
St Ignatius RC Primary School

BATTLE ATTACK

Battle is to begin, there's a bang on each drum
followed by toots on the trumpet.
Ball and chain, maces, swords and shields,
bow and arrow and daggers, both teams use as artillery.
Ball and chain in the left hand whilst the shield's in the other,
the same goes for the rest of the other artillery.
Bish, bash, bang, clash together the artillery and our armour suits.
Flesh ripping from our opponents' necks, you can almost hear
because of the our severe viciousness, triumphs over them.
The weather, bad as always when a battle like this is going on.
Our skill, strength, power and muscular strength mixed will win.
We're now the victors, just as I thought.

Andre John-Cave (11)
St Ignatius RC Primary School

THE SCOTTISH DRUM BEATS

The fierce battle is on,
Men stand face to face to fight in a savage way,
With swords and shields and daggers and balls,
The fight begins,
Campfires are lit giving a bright, shaded light,
To all fighters this night,
Women stand hand in hand, with tears running down their faces,
When the battle begins the sound effects roar,
The clash of the swords,
The beat of the drum is playing as the fighters fight.
Bloodstains on poor children's clothes,
One man raises his dagger high and Macbeth plunges him in his heart,
The crowd starts to cheer, some of them cry,
The beating of the drum starts again as the next battle begins.

Tara Clifford (11)
St Ignatius RC Primary School

BATTLE AGAINST EVIL

The battle had now begun.
Several people were injured and dozy.
People were grabbing onto the gungy mud,
struggling to pull themselves up the hills.
People were pushing upwards to keep their boots on.
The fierce battle had begun, with daggers.
Duncan, the king, was ahead of us
and I, Macbeth was in the middle.
As we walked up the hill more arrows started to fire upon us.
More and more people were getting injured every time.
They were also getting more dozy.
Inside I was praying for no more people to get injured.
I looked back and they were no longer gaining on us.

Elizabeth Charles (10)
St Ignatius RC Primary School

THE BATTLE

In the battle I could see heads dripping with blood like a fountain.
I was fighting with a man by the name of Ross,
His face was pouring with blood.
As I went back I threw my arrow at him and it hit his heart.
Down he fell covered with blood,
I, Macbeth, walked back for I could not look at such things.
I hit something very hard, hard like a stone.
I turned and I saw a man as big and mean as Goliath,
waiting steadily to fight with me.
He hit my sword and I hit his, hoping I was going to hit him.
He kept coming at me.
I couldn't see myself winning this big one.
I knew I had to do it for myself and the king.
So I took out my dagger and threw it at him and
another one went blood-rushingly down.
I, Macbeth, saw all the bodies that lay on the floor dying for our king.
We have won.
The victory is ours,
Glory, hallelujah,
Sing, sing, sing for our king!

Rebecca Ajala (11)
St Ignatius RC Primary School

AS THE BATTLE WENT ON

As the battle went on day by day, night by night,
many people lost their lives.

As many soldiers lost their boots and still walked
in the sloppy mud.

We went into battle face to face, with swords and
shields raised in the air.

Arrows and swords flying in the air screaming and
shouting over there.

Blood on swords, heads on floors, as the Scottish came
marching up.

The Scottish were strong, but we were stronger.

As the battle finished we had won and the Scottish
were no longer there.

Leon Azille (10)
St Ignatius RC Primary School

THE BIG BATTLE

As the beating went on all fighting, it was sad
All of them had swords, daggers, arrows and shields
They were all fighting it was a very hard war
They had to walk very far through the darkness and the yucky mud.
It was really bad and really scary
It was dark and stormy
The soldiers' hats kept falling off, they had metal protection
There was blood flying all over
It was really scary and most people died
There were swords going into people and daggers flying everywhere
The daggers were really sharp
And the swords and arrows had this poisonous thing
That is why people got killed
It was really sad and their boots had fallen off in the mud
Because it had dried up
It was the hardest war there ever was
Then, finally everyone died and it was over.

Tendai Chihota (11)
St Ignatius RC Primary School

MACBETH AT WAR

The night, I went to battle,
Was the night of blood and guts of people,
The most ghastly day of my life,
The mothers of scared children,
Waiting for the battle to start,
The men that I called enemies,
The men that looked into my eyes
Saying 'We will kill you,'
Then I drew my dagger at
The man they called John McCoy,
The fear in the children's eyes were unbearable, for words,
Then I could see him draw his dagger too,
Then I knew this was time for battle,
The drum started to beat a heavy tune,
I made the first move,
Then he made his,
I threw my dagger at him,
But it missed, I knew it was a silly thing to do,
All I had was my shield,
He had the eyes of sweet revenge,
But I knew he could not kill me,
I waited for him to come near,
When we came face to face I drew my bow and arrow,
I shot it through his heart,
As he died in agony not in peace,
Everyone gasped at the man who was my enemy,
Now dead at my feet.

Sinead Heenan (10)
St Ignatius RC Primary School

THE WAR

There's a sudden bang,
And everyone stops,
I can hear crying and weeping,
Drawn away through my ears,
As they struggle away from the thick,
sturdy, mud.

There's shooting and attacking,
Daggers in our faces
Crowds are yelling
Trying to make their lives longer.
But can they make it?

I watch people being killed in the war,
Blood dripping down their faces.
Suddenly there's a little cry,
I turn around,
To see a helpless child drowning in the mud.

Jennifer Odogwu (10)
St Ignatius RC Primary School

MACBETH AT BATTLE

This battle is really bloodthirsty.
Thy fled with thy swords
Shalt never like to be in war,
The fierce fighting of thou swords.
Clish, clash, wish, wash!
Thee thy have come to fight
With their bow and arrows and vicious swords,
Thy have come to start a battle.
With a clash of my sword I killed my enemy,
There was a loud *bash!* As he fell to the ground.

Louise James (10)
St Ignatius RC Primary School

BATTLE SOUNDS

'Conquer!'
Shouts our king.
The war, I Macbeth
For him, will win.

'Attack!'
Shouts the enemy.
But to us,
It is their death decree.

Bang!
The drummer beats the drum.
The Scottish are at war,
I am among.

Clang!
Goes my sword against his shield.
Me thinks he is winning,
But soon he will be killed.

Thud!
I have pushed him to the ground.
I have to kill him, my heart beats,
Making a throbbing sound.

Slash!
I cut off his head.
We are near victory,
Another enemy is dead.

'Hail!'
Through the fields our voices ring.
We have won the battle,
We did it for our king.

Esther Kuforiji (11)
St Ignatius RC Primary School

PEACE

In all the countries there should be peace
At ease
Especially those who fight
With all might
We want peace
Let's cease
What is not fair?
Is war getting rough in the air?
Let's stop fighting and war
And have some peace
Peace, peace, peace
Ease, ease, ease
We all need celebrations
In all the nations
Fight, fight, fight
Is always a bad night
Kill, kill, kill
Comes out ill
War, war, war
Turns out as 'ar'
Don't do something you would regret
Or you won't forgive on earth.

Ogechi Ekeanyanwu (11)
St Ignatius RC Primary School

MY HAND

Hands feel very smooth, my nails are very dry.
My veins are colours of red, blue, white, purple, yellow
On my hands I see shapes of squares, twirls and circles and even more.
My favourite thing to touch is food.
I don't like touching sharks or they will eat you alive.

Conor McCarthy (9)
St Martin of Porres RC Primary School

EVENING SOUNDS

When I come home from school
this is what I hear . . .

My sister playing -
diddle de dum.
The TV -
chatter, chat, chatter.

People walking -
clatter, tap, clatter
The washing machine -
tubble, tubble, tubble

My mum making the dinner -
boil, boil, boil
Cars parking outside -
brum, brum.

As I wait for the darkness
that is what I hear.

Rebecca O'Donoghue (9)
St Martin of Porres RC Primary School

THE LUMBERING ELE . . .

The shadowy silhouette
    Walking across the sunset,
Glistening against the water,
    Moving slowly across the
Hot, cracked land.
    His watery eyes are alert,
His big floppy ears are listening
    The timid animals make way for him just like a king.

Charlotte Webb (11)
St Martin of Porres RC Primary School

THE KING OF NIGHTMARES

Go on into your nightmares . . .

You run through lashing corn entwining your feet.
You race, the leaves dancing gracefully but menacingly,
encircling you in a wreath of yellow and orange.
You duck and dodge under whipping branches which want to whip you,
You skip through a sea of grass, swishing like waves, tripping you up.
The towering trees swaying and howling like werewolves.
The rain needles pricking you, and penetrating right through your skin.
You run and run screaming whilst dodging buildings
                                        crashing to the ground.
Suddenly you see a tall wall of ashen clouds, and on the other side,
                        the wondrous yellow of the good dream world.
A gloomy cloud swishes down and you climb onto it.
This is a one way ticket to see the king of nightmares . . . the wind!

Lora Allen-Bortolotti (11)
St Martin of Porres RC Primary School

THE BORDER COLLIE

Its black and white fur glistening in the sun of the countryside.
It bounds along in the grassy fields.
The way it moves gracefully along.
The way it looks around looking for something to get up to.
The energy it has could keep it going for hours.
Its cute face with such pleading eyes.
Its bushy tail swaying from side to side.
It is lovely to feel its smooth silky forehead.
Its rough tongue leaving a great wet mark right across your face.
Its gentle way of playing with you,
Even though it can pin you down with one leap.
They are very intelligent and also very cunning creatures.

Matthew Carter (11)
St Martin of Porres RC Primary School

PREDATOR

Touch it if you dare,
Surely it would be your worst nightmare.
Feel the vibrations as it lumbers past.
Its beady yellow eyes flicker fast.
T-Rex, king of lizards, the mighty one.
Those predatorial claws glisten,
Its prey listens and shows its blood-drenched horns
Beast and beast rumble and tumble
T-Rex gets injured, roars out loud,
And frightens the crowd.
A slash from a claw, a graze from a talon
And it opens its mouth wide.
And another bloodcurdling sound is heard.

Olivier Goder (10)
St Martin of Porres RC Primary School

HANDS

Hands are smooth,
Hands are rough,
Hands are hard,
Hands are soft,
Hands are even wrinkly,
Hands are tough,
Hands are baggy,
Hands are dry,
Hands are greasy,
Hands are even flaky,
Hands are clay-like,
Hands are flexible.

Carl Bleach (9)
St Martin of Porres RC Primary School

SCORPION FISH

A scorpion fish can camouflage,
yet again it isn't that large.
It can be yellow, brown, green,
orange or blue.
It can even poison you!
It is very slim and has big long legs,
It jumps around from hedge to hedge
On its tail are deadly sharp spikes,
You'd better beware, it does what it likes.
It lives in the tropical waters inside the coral reef,
and humans come along and give the fish more and more grief.
It isn't a friendly creature and prefers to be alone!
Humans are coming along now and killing their home, the coral reef.
So the scorpion fish are dying and like I said,
receiving more and more grief!

Natalie Carolan (10)
St Martin of Porres RC Primary School

THE RUSTLING WIND

Watch the wind how it sends the leaves dancing.
Whooshing past the trees sending them flying.
In the morning it is chilly.
In the night it is cold and bitter.
The wind is strong and powerful so it makes the trees sway.
As the wind pushes you like you are going to fall over.

Rachel Paul (11)
St Martin of Porres RC Primary School

SOUNDS AROUND THE SCHOOL

I hear sounds around my head
This is what I hear,
Children screaming,
Giggling, moaning.
Chalk screeching
Pencils breaking
Rulers snapping
Sharpeners crunching

Why are there so many
sounds around
my school
today?

Christina Donellan (9)
St Martin of Porres RC Primary School

A POEM FOR MY MUM

My mum is so loving,
My mum buys me sweets,
My mum buys me chocolate,
Such delightful treats.

My mum takes care of me,
Every night and day,
And even when the clouds go by,
up and away.

God please take care of my mum
because she is a person to love.

Sean Hamill (8)
St Martin of Porres RC Primary School

REEF STINGRAY

He's flat, smooth and spotty,
His food is disappearing fast.
He can grow to a hundred centimetres,
So beware or else.
He lives with tropical fish,
And he would eat from divers' hands,
So long as he's got food.
He's wavy, rippled and up and down,
His sting will hurt so keep away.
His eyes are disgustingly yellow,
And big and bulgy too.
He swims away like the wind at day.

> So keep away
> from the reef
> stingray.

Matthew Clifford (10)
St Martin of Porres RC Primary School

MY HANDS AND YOUR HANDS

Every hand is special and very unique
because your veins flow down your hand like a river.
Hands like scary things, like pumpkin pie,
Or give things like garlands of flowers
to a special person that you really, really like.
Maybe your hands have shapes like squares, ovals and circles
but the colours in my hands are orange, red and purple.

Iain Quin (9)
St Martin of Porres RC Primary School

HANDS

My hands are brown
they are soft
and my hands are smooth
and they have tops
and they are peach
and they are green
and they have lines going across
and they are reddish
and I can see snarly lines
and I can see through them
and I can see white
and I can see that my hands
are strong.

Jonathan Ofume (9)
St Martin of Porres RC Primary School

BAD WIND

The wind blows strong
The trees begin to tremble
The leaves follow
The wind is evil
So he hides from us
He sings, he shouts
We go for cover
Soon all is hushed
The sun comes out
We rejoice
And the wind comes again.

Keegan Webb (9)
St Martin of Porres RC Primary School

SOUNDS AROUND SCHOOL

In my classroom you can find
All the children laughing and chattering.
The register calling name by name,
Until my name was finally called.
The teacher shouting.
The chalk scratching, sharpeners crunching
Pencils breaking
Boy life is tough!

The playground is even noisier!
So let's take a look at the sounds they make.
Bell ringing, children screaming.
Feet stamping, children moaning.
People singing, children shouting,
Children giggling
Rattle goes the fence.
All this makes me hungry
Let's take a little trip to the hall.

In the hall you can hear
Folks scratching, plates clattering
Water splashing.
Ball bouncing, whistle blowing.
Children singing.
Don't mind me I've got a letter
to put in the office.

In the office you can hear
Phone ringing, typewriter clattering,
Intercom buzzer buzzing away.

So that's my five hour poem about sounds
around school.
I hope I will see you later.

Daniel Rassaby (9)
St Martin of Porres RC Primary School

SCALEFIN ANTHIAS

Look at captivating colours enriched in skin,
They look as if surrounded in an Atlantic world
Beneath our comprehension
Look at the golden scalefin swim past,
The golden sunset into the water's reflection.

They socially work as a team
In sunset beam,
But when the sun goes down they
Wear a frown,
For today our petite fishes
Will stop work and say
Good Night!

Leslie Selormey-Addy (10)
St Martin of Porres RC Primary School

HANDS

My hands are soft and smooth.

My hands are like lakes and rivers
of blue, red, purple, green and white
in the night.

My hands are feathers in the wind.
My hands are like a night lake graze.

My hands overflow with beauty and grace,
I really love my hands at this pace!

Emma Holtom (8)
St Martin of Porres RC Primary School

HANDS

My hands are twirly, like a whirlpool in the sea;
My fingers are unique and belong to me!

If you feel my skin, it is quite smooth;
But my hands have got some indents,
Not forgetting the groove.

My groove and my lines are like train tracks;
My hands are supple, up to the max!

I like my hands, for me they are true;
It's the same for your hands, they belong to you.

Joe Riordan (9)
St Martin of Porres RC Primary School

ME

I'm as tall as a giraffe,
Fast as a cheetah
As proud as a peacock
As brave as a lion
As strong as an ox
I can sing, dance, and act on TV
I can do all sports
I'm as agile as a monkey
Gentle as a lamb
But when it comes to it,
I will scare you as much as I can.

David Kelly (10)
St Martin of Porres RC Primary School

THE WIND

In the night the wind blows,
Swishing, whooshing,
All around.

In the night the wind fights,
Rough and tough,
Round and round.

In the night the wind roars,
Through and through,
The leaves of trees.

In the night the wind is powerful,
With the strength of strength
Of the mighty Jupiter.

In the night, the middle of the night,
The wind calmly goes down
With the softness gently going, going and going.

Emily De Maria (9)
St Martin of Porres RC Primary School

COLOUR ON PEOPLE'S HANDS

Blue for the veins,
Red for blood,
Purple for scar,
Yellow for the palms of your hands,
White is for your nails,
Peach is for your skin.

Sinead Whitney (9)
St Martin of Porres RC Primary School

WHAT'S THAT?

Bang, bang! What was that? Only the wind,
Do I hear wolves?
No that's the wind,
Why do I think I'm falling over?
No that's the wind,
Even though I feel you,
Why can I not see you?
Are you dead or are you an alien?
Creak, crack
What was that?
Will doom, doom blow me away?
Please don't blow me away!
Why don't you blow away America?
Fear the windows are here, or you could
                    swirl and twirl me around,
In a snap of your foot.
Your breath might destroy the Earth!
Rustle, rustle, what was that?

Jonathan Kay (9)
St Martin of Porres RC Primary School

PEOPLE'S HANDS

Some people's hands are soft.
Some people's hands are rough.
Some people's hands are flexible.
But mine are just right!
Some people's hands are baggy.
Some people's hands are greasy.
Some people's hands are smooth and rough.
But mine are just wrinkly.

Veronica Owysy Nyantakyiwa (9)
St Martin of Porres RC Primary School

THE HORRIBLE RAIN

Rain why do you wet me?
Why do you drip through holes?
Why do you make babies cry?
Why don't you go away
And let the sun come out?
Why are people so wet
When they're outside
But inside people feel damp and soggy?

Rain do you have to come?
Why don't you go some other place
Somewhere far away?
Why do you have to come here,
Please go away and never come back again
Ever, ever again.

Hannah Ely Taylor (10)
St Martin of Porres RC Primary School

MY HANDS

My hands are special to me
Smooth sometimes, hard sometimes
Brilliant all the time
I like my hands
They're like a friend to me
I like my hands because
I can win games
Get house points
I love my hands!

Joseph Gomes (9)
St Martin of Porres RC Primary School

I WISH I DIDN'T EXIST

I sit beside the tree every day
thinking that I'm invisible
or I'm just a thing
but I'm not, I'm no one.

I'd stay there all night long
still feeling forgotten and depressed.

I feel ashamed sometimes for nothing
but I just feel like that
for I'm just nothing.

There's a playground behind me
but if I go in no one will notice me
for I'm just nothing.

Susan O'Toole (9)
St Martin of Porres RC Primary School

BABY HANDS

Baby hands are very small
Not like ours, which are quite tall
Baby hands are soft and smooth
Flexible and always on the move
Baby hands are not rough
And definitely not very tough
But my hands are rough and dry
Why are they different? I don't know why.

Jonathan Nunn (8)
St Martin of Porres RC Primary School

AUTUMN DAYS

Autumn days when the leaves are coloured
And the acorn is in its little shell.
Clocks go back and the nights get longer
And the heating bill goes up!

Autumn days when animals are getting ready
Getting ready to hibernate
The apples are falling and the berries are ripening
And the fire gets turned on full time.

Autumn days when your clothes are getting warmer
And the leaves are shrinking and I am growing.
Time for the magical beasts to appear
So keep inside and be careful!

Emilia Berni (10)
St Martin of Porres RC Primary School

HANDS, HANDS

Hands, hands, wonderful hands
Think how hard it would be without our wonderful hands.
Some hands are wrinkly and old
Some hands are soft and smooth
But my hands are dry, dry and bony, bony and hairy.
Some hands are small
Some hands are big
But my hands are very nice and I like them the way they are.

Bobo Ahmed (8)
St Martin of Porres RC Primary School

THE PUFFER-FISH

Japanese like to eat this fish,
They think it's a real treat,
But do they know the liver holds,
A killing filling not nice to eat.

This fish is fat, with eyes to go with it,
Its food is very small.

It lives in the coral reef
And looks as if it's got no teeth.

It can blow itself up to keep itself safe
But once this is done its life is gone.

After that it's probably not fat
It is turned into an ornament or a lampshade
But that's not nice, don't you agree?

So if you see a puffer-fish
Just leave it be.

Greg Hamlin (10)
St Martin of Porres RC Primary School

THE SHAPED HAND

The hands circle like a sun.
So many squares like incy, wincy buildings.
The shaped hands have circles.
But my hands are just little normal hands.
The big hands have big 'O' loops in them.
But we have no 'O' loops in ours.

Kade Francis (8)
St Martin of Porres RC Primary School

HANDS

Hands are very useful,
They help us eat and play
Some are silky, some are dry,
Some are fragile and delicate,
Some hands are scaly,
Some hands are very long and thick,
And sometimes are as long as a stick,
People's hands are scarred,
People's hands are veined,
But my hands are soft and smooth,
Just like a bunny's tail
Hands may be hairy
Hands may be flexible
Hands are all unique.

Emily Jane Crampton (11)
St Martin of Porres RC Primary School

MY HANDS

Hands are rough, hands are soft.
And hands are like loops,
hands have baggy parts.
But best of all hands are flexible.
Hands are blue,
hands are red and hands are white.
But best of all hands are pink.
Hands are dagger-like.
Hands are curvy,
but the best hands are square.

Garvan Seaman (9)
St Martin of Porres RC Primary School

Rain!

It was a nice sunny day and I was going to the park with some friends.
Then I felt a sudden perishing moist trickle down my back.
The silky rain so tender runs down my finger,
Like the wax on a candle.
I feel the harsh rain splash on my finger
As it falls to the ground the soapy rain builds a stream
Running across the road, the stream seems to go on forever.
Like the sky so high.
The pounding rain is now soaking me to the bone
From head to toe, I shiver as once again I feel
The silky rain, so tender running down my finger
Like the wax on a candle.

Jade Rolph (9)
St Martin of Porres RC Primary School

The Old Hand

There was an old hand which was very wrinkly,
And when it tickled me it was quite tingly.
It had lots of spots you would think it had chicken pox.
It has lots of shapes,
these are the ones it makes . . .
Lots of life-lines and some circles,
rectangles and triangles too.
I think old hands are quite scary,
They're probably like Granny Mary's.

Barbara Yiapanis (8)
St Martin of Porres RC Primary School

Wet, Wet, Wet

It started off as drip, drip, drip sounds
But then it started to come down a bit more heavier
It started off as drip, drip, drip sounds
But then the drops seemed to get bigger.

It started off as drip, drip, drip sounds
But then little puddles formed
It started off as drip, drip, drip sounds
But then I felt quite heavy rain on my nose.

It started off as drip, drip, drip sounds
But then it started to pour
It started off as drip, drip, drip sounds
But by then I was soaked head to toe.

Tolga Kiamil (9)
St Martin of Porres RC Primary School

Alone

There I was one day in the park left alone
                              and feeling abandoned
Because no one would play with me,
Nobody to talk to just alone feeling lonely,
Forgotten, not in this world any more.
I feel like I've done something wrong
But in my heart I know I haven't,
When I try to join in all they do is just
                              ignore me.

Isabella Spagnuolo (10)
St Martin of Porres RC Primary School

THE HAND

The hand was as flat as a pancake,
With protruding veins sticking out,
The fingers were all different
Two were chubby and short,
The thumbs were hairy and wide,
The rest were all the same really,
Long and wrinkled they were.

The palm of the hand was as hot as a boil,
It was red as a tomato as well,
It had a freckle in the middle,
With short little lines around it,
It had a few scars here and there.

Apart from all of these things,
The hand was really quite nice,
It was moist, all flexible
As a gymnast's hand,
It was also very pale.

Rachel McCormack (11)
St Martin of Porres RC Primary School

ME

I like football, tennis, swimming too
I like running but I am not sure if I am going or coming,
I like my bike. I've got a godfather Mike.
I like my girlfriend she's very fine and we're both nine.
I like pizza, pasta, pitta bread too
I like vegetables, fruit, different things
Forgettable or not.

Christopher Silva (10)
St Martin of Porres RC Primary School

CHRISTMAS TIME

In a stable far away, is a baby
Cold in winter's wind.
Icy days will go away
All the children wait in December
For Christmas Day
Hip, hip, hooray, they all shout
For three days to go
As they play in winter's snow
For soon we will celebrate
The birth of a child
Who saved us but died.
In a stable far away, is a baby
Cold in winter's wind.

Ruben Tojeiro-Gonzalez (10)
St Martin of Porres RC Primary School

THE REEF STINGRAY

His spotty, spread out, smooth, wiggly body
Moves swiftly across the sand,
Showing off his threatening tail
Warning you if you harm him he will
Strike you with that poisonous tail.
His yellow, beady little eyes are spying for some grub,
He will spring out and eat you in one gulp.
When it's time for him to sleep he hides under the sand,
He says goodnight everyone I'll be back tomorrow!

Xenia Savva (9)
St Martin of Porres RC Primary School

RAIN

The rain is splashing, splishing, sploshing,
It's dripping in a spray.
The rain is clammy and washing,
All the chalk away.

It's slowing down a bit,
It's nearly stopping. Yeah!
It's really delicate and soft too.

It's stopped!

It's sunny now,
The weather is deceptive.
All the children go out to play,
And draw and play hopscotch again!

Corinne Quaid (10)
St Martin of Porres RC Primary School

SHARKY BOY

My best friend Sharky Boy
Is black and grey and blue.
Sharky Boy has some bad press
But even so I must confess
He is not the prettiest thing I've ever seen
Swimming round the waters green
Looking for food.
The mood that he is usually in is fairly good.
Especially when he has had a meal,
Of tasty fish and sea lions!

Connie Pugh (10)
St Martin of Porres RC Primary School

POEM OF THE WIND

Hear the wind outside roaring and roaring,
Then suddenly I wake up from my awful snoring,
I look outside as the wind goes on.
Then I feel frightened and the wind sings a song.
Whistling and whispering
Its big old hands banging on the garden shed.
I jump back into my little old bed
Then it swirls round the big old trees.
Then it starts stacking in and out the leaves
Then I think of roaring and roaring
And I go back to my awful old snoring.

Rachel O'Donnell (10)
St Martin of Porres RC Primary School

THE HORSE THAT WAS WOODEN

The horse that was wooden was cool,
He had sunglasses and sat on a stool.
He was ten meters long and stood oblong,
With his feet on a stool he was cool.

The horse that was wooden was the best,
Because he wore a vest on top of his chest.
He was so brave he made a cave
Which was so steep it was an antique.

Jack Palczewski (10)
St Martin of Porres RC Primary School

HAWKFISH

Of white and brown,
Spots and blobs.

Of rich habitats,
Made full of reefs.

They move slowly, slowly,
But careful though.

Be careful in the morning
Because you can be a hawkfish's
Dinner!

Cristina Moglia (9)
St Martin of Porres RC Primary School

OLD HANDS

Wrinkly, freckly, rough, old hands,
Old age has come and will expand,
You can see through the years where old
                                hands were not
But young hands no longer see the plot
Curvy, scaly, bony old hands,
Some might think of elastic bands
And some might think of forbidden lands
But I myself think old hands are good,
For they've been through what others should.

Chantal Benett (10)
St Martin of Porres RC Primary School

TORTOISE

His little quiet feet making heavy steps
As he walks to a cool place.
He finds a place and has a rest.
Morning comes and he goes off to find some food
Through the open fields he goes
He finds a piece of lettuce
His eyes water and he puts his mouth around the piece of food
Then finally he takes a chunk of the lettuce and chews
It's night time now so he goes back and digs a hole
And wraps himself up nice and warm for winter to pass.

Anthony Wentworth (10)
St Martin of Porres RC Primary School

WHITE

What is white, a shining colour that sparkles on the moon
The colour of clouds in the sky
The colour of paper that you write on
The colour of paint
And also the colour of cars on the road
The colour of snow,
The colour of milk
And the colour of a swan
The colour of vanilla,
And it is the sign of winter.

James Geraghty (11)
St Martin of Porres RC Primary School

A MYSTERY COLOUR

The mystery colour I am telling you
Maybe is the colour that would suit you.
It is a colour you might lend
It maybe in the new trend
It is lighter than light
Or powerful as might.
It may be dark it may be light
It might give us all a great big fright
It may be a colour, it might not
But it is better than being shot
The colour I talk of is gold.

John McCoy (10)
St Martin of Porres RC Primary School

WHAT IS GREEN

Green is the grass blowing in the wind
Green are the leaves dancing all day long
Green is the colour of bushes wobbling about.

What is green, nobody knows
Green is the colour of frogs jumping up and down
Green is the colour of a packet of crisps.

What is green, nobody knows.
Green is the colour of books.
Green is the colour of a tray being lifted.

Linda Pham (10)
St Martin of Porres RC Primary School

THE SEA

The sea can be rough or calm,
You never know how it will act.
The waves when the sea is rough are as ferocious as a lion.
The waves when the sea is calm are as friendly as a soft toy
The sea is more almighty than a million men.
It can lash out and whip back in a flash,
It can lash out and whip back in a year.
The sea is uncontrollable.
And I hope it will stay that way forever,
I like the sea because it is good to me.

Shan Hiu (11)
St Martin of Porres RC Primary School

THE SEA

The sea can be crashing, almighty and powerful
The sea can be gentle, peaceful and smooth.
Its colours look beautiful until it lashes out.
With its pale grey and its dark sea blue
You won't notice it until it comes for you
But sometimes I don't like it when it's very tall
But when it's banging and loud I don't like it at all
But one day when I see it, it shouldn't be too bad
And I should like it a bit.

Laurie Marie Thompson (11)
St Martin of Porres RC Primary School

AUTUMN DAYS

Autumn days when the leaves fall down
Down, down, down to the ground
Scarlet, hazel and golden brown.

Leaves are scattered everywhere
Amber here and red over there.

Crunch, crunch, go the leaves when you're passing by
Autumn's here again you sigh!

Leaves are scattered everywhere
Amber here and red over there.

The wind whistles by and
The rain patters down
And the grey sky seems to frown.

Leaves are scattered everywhere
Amber here and red over there.

Sarah Monaghan (10)
St Martin of Porres RC Primary School

ALMIGHTY SEA

The almighty sea is cracking the rocks.
The hands of the sea are pulling me from the shore.
The waves relentless and the foam is on the beach.
The sand and the shells are washed to sea.
The water clashes with the wind.
The waves ride up on the beach.
The wind whistling while the sea rides along the shore.
The colours of the sea are grey, green, white and blue.

Kevin Cooley (10)
St Martin of Porres RC Primary School

DRIP, DRIP OF THE RAIN

The rain went past, gentle as a fly
The thick heavy clouds were in the sky.

The trickle of the rain made everybody tickle!

The soft rain goes pitter, patter
The rain falls down and makes a clatter.

The rain swoops and swirls, curls and twirls.

Drip, drop the rain has stopped.

Annie Duggan (10)
St Martin of Porres RC Primary School

I HEARD THE WIND

I heard the wind rustling by me,
Trying to tell me what to do.
It didn't like me because it could not blow me
I looked up at the dark blue sky
And the snow white clouds
And the burning hot sun, making my face roast.
Here it comes again rushing past me
It feels like a haunting shiver rushing past,
It gives up and just sways past me
I look down and see the leaves dancing around my feet.

Sinead O'Neill (11)
St Martin of Porres RC Primary School

HANDS

There he stood looking straight at his hands in front of him,
They were dry, wrinkly, hard and spotty
He looked at somebody else's hands
They were big, tight, tough and tanned.
Then he looked at somebody else's hands
They were large, clean, elegant and freckled,
Then he looked at his hands
And thought to himself will my hands ever change?

Marco Varani (10)
St Martin of Porres RC Primary School

THE POLAR BEAR

The polar bear is as white as glistening snow,
He is big and fierce and growls a lot,
The silky fur as soft as cotton and wool,
It has a very big nose but has very small eyes,
It has a bit of padding on its hands and feet,
It will not grow cold because it has a big furry coat,
Its ears are quite small but they are not as big as its nose.

Claire Whitney (11)
St Martin of Porres RC Primary School

THE HAND

The tips of the fingers are red and stubby.
The palm of the hand is small and chubby.
The hand is flabby, sweaty and tight.
The hand is scaly and a very beautiful sight.
The hand is yellowish, dead and thick.
From far away the fingers look like little carrot sticks.

Larissa Attisso (11)
St Martin of Porres RC Primary School

PANDA

The panda is big black and white
He lives in the mountains they are big green and white
He eats bamboo all day and all night
A panda looks cute and cuddly but,
Don't touch, he'll turn in spite
He runs through the mountains as he searches for prey
He carries on running till the end of the day
As the night falls his eyes shine like stars
In the dark black night.

Meghann O'Brien (11)
St Martin of Porres RC Primary School

HANDS

Hands are useful,
Nearly all the time,
Hands are delicate and fragile,
Hands are unique,
In all that you do,
Even if you had a twin
They'd still be like you,
Hands are small,
Hands are big.

Alexandra Jane Hollis (11)
St Martin of Porres RC Primary School

WILD SEA

The wild sea
As the morning comes up the sea starts to get rough
And the sky starts to go as black as smoke.
It's as cold as ice
Sometimes as strong as the wind
But as it gets to the top
You can hear it banging against the walls.
When the afternoon comes
The sea goes as soft as a baby's face
And as the evening comes on
The sea goes as calm as a pond.

Le-Le Elias (10)
St Martin of Porres RC Primary School

TO A NEW-BORN BABY

I will give the baby peace in its life.
I will bring him a candle so his life
Will be bright and filled with sunshine.
I will give him all the gold I have,
For his heart will always be pure like gold.
I will grant the baby love,
For the baby will be full of love in its heart.
I shall bring the baby the world,
So he will have good friends.
I give the baby my happiness,
So he will be filled with joy.
If I ever see this baby,
I will never let him out of my arms.

Florence Akinwunmi (11)
St Mary's RC Junior School

THE SKY

The sky called my name,
With a smile on its face.
I looked up with delight,
My feeling, so bright.

He said, 'Hey, Anita come
Join us up here.'
I said, 'Sky how can I,
It's so high up there?'

He said, 'Hey, Anita,
Don't worry my friend,
I'll lift you up,
With my big cloudy hand.'

I met his cloud friends
As he lifted me high,
And I joined him up there,
High in the sky.

Anita Keshi (11)
St Mary's RC Junior School

SNOW

Snowflakes are like pearls
Fun to play with and make
Your hands glow
Now come on children
Play with the snow
It is not like a lump of coal
It is fun like a ton of gold.

Darren O'Brien (11)
St Mary's RC Junior School

THE WINTER SNOW

Snow is white
As a sheet of paper
It's like paint
Covering a dark ground
Making it smooth.

Like washing-up liquid
Cleaning the dirt
Off plates and cups
It's magic powder
Falling smoothly
On rough streets
Changing them
Into beautiful carpets.

Stasio Mickiewicz (11)
St Mary's RC Junior School

STAR

A star which gleams
Like an eye in the night
A gem so crystal clear
Lonely in its space
Bold and gold
Like a mirror shining down
How I wonder on those cat nights
Is there life high up there?

Carlo Capuno (11)
St Mary's RC Junior School

TO BABY ELISA

I'll bring you a candle
To remind you that Jesus
Is the light of the world

I have brought you a globe
To remind you that
The world is your home

I wish you a tiger
So when you'll grow up
You'll be strong and wise

I'll give you music
So you can sing
As sweet as a bird

I'll grant you love
So you can grow up with
Love all around you

But best of all
I've given you life
Surrounded by people who love.

Michelle Licheri (10)
St Mary's RC Junior School

STRANGE ALIENS

Mysterious aliens,
Like unsolved questions.
As strange as disappearing ghosts.
Their flying saucers are like scrunched up paper.
We will one day know the truth.

Khoi Nguyen (11)
St Mary's RC Junior School

TRANSPORT

The rubbish collector is like a monster
Which devours our thrown out things
Roaring down the street
Eating anything in sight
Its human servants feed it all day long
Till it's big and fat

A plane is like a bullet
Shooting from country to country
From the ground it seems to float
Up there it moves like lightning

The HGV thunders along
As if it's the king of the road
Don't mess with this beast
It won't follow the Highway Code.

Morgan Hamilton-Griffin (11)
St Mary's RC Junior School

MY SON

I bring a book for you to learn
I give you my heart for eternal life
I give you a seed for growth
You shall be king
I give you a lion for courage
I grant you the light of the world.

John Bailey (10)
St Mary's RC Junior School

A HEART FULL OF LOVE

A heart is like a pot of gold
At the other end of the rainbow
To be true and faithful
Listen to what your heart has to say.

A heart is your true guide
Guides you in the right place
If you listen to your heart
You can hear it saying
Relax and be soft as a rose
For you are a child of God.

A heart is as light as a rose
And as loveable as love can be
Your heart is a truthful thing.

Sarah Nicholas (10)
St Mary's RC Junior School

AIR

The smell of sweet air
Like perfume
You sniff the air
Like a dog searching for prey
You are swept along
Like a spinning windmill
The chill runs through your body
And the air flies across you
Like a fan on full speed.

Angela Isojeh (10)
St Mary's RC Junior School

THE RING OF GOLD

The ring of gold,
Glimmers in the sun,
Shimmers in the sea,
Oh what a warm feeling,
It gives me.

The ring of gold,
It is so old,
It holds secrets,
Never told,
Oh what a warm feeling,
It gives me.

The ring of gold,
Must now unfold,
For it must entwine,
My life with yours,
Oh what a warm feeling,
It gives me.

Debbie Wilton (11)
St Mary's RC Junior School

IN SPACE

The moon is as
Round as a football
The stars shine
Like specks of gold
The darkness is like
A hole in the ground.

Matthew Crosby (11)
St Mary's RC Junior School

AFRICA

I know a world
A wondrous world
Feeding with milk
And honey

I know a world
A world of culture,
Education
And manufacturers

I know a world
A world of peace and laws
Full of animals
It is Africa.

Anthony Chukwuma (11)
St Mary's RC Junior School

MATCH OF THE DAY

The whistle goes
The battle starts
The crowd chanting like an army
Going into war
The captain yelling, 'Get that ball.'
Balls fired like bullets
Goal! Goal! Goal!
The final whistle 2-1
The war continues.

Karl Lett (11)
St Mary's RC Junior School

THE GRANDFATHER CLOCK

The grandfather clock
Struck a rhythm in my head.
The pendulum swung from side to side
Like a conductor keeping the beat.

The clock played his lonely note,
As each of the hours passed.
He stood sad and alone,
And chimed a forlorn tune.

The clock stood listening
To whispered secrets of generations
And as each of the hours chimed
He let a secret out!

Hanna McBride (11)
St Mary's RC Junior School

THE SEA

The sea was angry
Like a volcano ready to erupt
White foam spat off the rocks.
The fish below
Were thrown to and fro
Like leaves blowing in the wind.

Glen Howard (10)
St Mary's RC Junior School

THE SPACE SHUTTLE

The space shuttle stared into the lonely sky,
Wondering how long it would be until they met.
When they met, what would they do?
Maybe, glide together side by side,
And tell stories of each other's worlds!
But then the space shuttle would fly,
Up into space, away from earth.
That would be exciting!
Exploring space, and stopping by to see the moon!
The space shuttle is waiting,
At any moment, it will take off,
Into the sky!

Anabel Calvelo (11)
St Mary's RC Junior School

THE RIVER

The river flows through the peaceful land,
It sparkles in the sun.
Giving it the reflection of chilled white wine,
Straight from the fridge.
The animals of the forest have gathered,
To drink the water that will refresh them,
And make them feel relieved.

Emily Osei-Blavo (11)
St Mary's RC Junior School

To My Son

I wish you to be
As clever as an owl,
As funny as a hyena,
As strong as a gorilla

As fast as a gazelle,
As responsible as a lion,
As healthy as a kangaroo,
As good as an ostrich,
And as co-operative as a dog,

But even if you aren't
Any of these things
I'll still love you
Because you are my son.

Olawale Peter Olafisoye (11)
St Mary's RC Junior School

To An Unknown Baby

I bring you love to remind you
That we love you all the time
I give you light to remind you
Of the light of the world
I will be with you for a long time
So you will get to know me better.

Tony Harnett (10)
St Mary's RC Junior School

TO BABY EMMA

I bring you a seed so you
Can grow to love others,
I grant you talent,
I have brought you the sun,
So you shall be bright,
I wish for you to have friends,
Now I wish for you to have
A healthy and happy life.

Teresa McKinney (11)
St Mary's RC Junior School

RAIN

Rain is like a streak of silver
Falling in the world's whirlwind
Falling on my window-pane
How refreshing is the rain
After the dusty summer heat
The children are locked away
Smudging the window
With their sad breath.

Sarah Allen (11)
St Mary's RC Junior School

STARS

The night was filled with a thousand eyes,
Crying tears of pain and anger,
Weeping balls of light,
In the funeral of space.

Twinkling bombs of World War 2
Silent memories locked away,
A glitter in the empty sky,
Where German bombers would have flown.

Shimmering candles,
Cloaked in black,
Like monks they stand,
But, one dream and they fade.

The icy black of midnight comes,
And, like army lights, they follow,
They never go anywhere,
But wait to welcome the morning home.

Light of heaven,
Like gold they are,
Shimmering, shining, glittering,
The sacred fire of the sky.

Lucy Dobson (11)
St Mary's RC Junior School

HOW COME?

How come when you
Come down stairs
Your mum says,
'What do you want for breakfast?'

How come when you
Come to school
The road is always busy?

How come when you
Do something bad
You wish you'd never done it?

How come when you
Turn around
You feel quite dizzy.

Jodie Pinchion (9)
St Michael At Bowes Junior School

THE BLUE FLOWER

Under the trees
over the hill
and far away
the blue flower lays.
Swinging in the breeze
left and right
and it's never been found.

Michael Loukoumis (9)
St Michael At Bowes Junior School

THE TEACHER'S LOUNGE

There was a teacher's lounge.
The lounge was very big
It had a busted coffee
machine and a
toilet with a
pig.

Dimitra Stylianou (9)
St Michael At Bowes Junior School

I DRIFT AWAY

As I gaze in depression out of the cold, misty
Window that hides the moonlight.
I see the dark black duvet that holds the glittering
diamonds that lead me to my future. As I watch
I wonder, I drift away into a dream that carries
me ahead, I see God's hand guiding me to a
place where no living thing has gone.
Then I drift back again, to know
my future death.

Nalân Burgess (8)
St Michael's Primary School, Highgate

STARS

Gleaming red Mars,
Just a bit brighter,
Then as bright as
The gleaming gold stars.
As bright as a sunflower.

Almost everywhere around you,
Stars, planets,
The most sparkling thing ever seen,
The sun, burning your eyes so much,
You can barely see
Like you're in a room full of sunflowers.

No humans around you, no nothing.
Just gleaming stars and planets,
The brightest things ever.
The brightest things there ever will be!

James Davies (8)
St Michael's Primary School, Highgate

COSMIC IS COSMIC

The sun breathes hot air for earth
The earth spins like a child's spinning top.
The nice green turf
I'm as round as a lollipop.
The stars appear like diamonds on black silk.
Everyone likes me.
Blue is mainly sky and sea.
Can't you see -
I'm a home!

Karima Dakhama (8)
St Michael's Primary School, Highgate

COSMOS

I was there at the beginning,
When Greek myths were told,
Lots of things have changed now,
But I'm still getting old.
I looked out of the telescope,
for the first time in my life
and asked myself some cosmology questions,
a few of which I will mention.
Is the universe the same everywhere?
How did the universe begin?
Will the universe go on the same way forever?

These questions I have been wondering about
for a long time and hope, some day to find the answer.

Emma Tulloch (10)
St Michael's Primary School, Highgate

MYSTERIOUS SPACE

I am in space.
I see an ugly face.
It is an alien.
It could be an Australian.
It has three eyes and a nose
The eyes look like a hose.
I think it says 'Hello'
But you'll never know.
I can see lots of stars
I can also see Mars.
I can see craters here
Some aliens can appear.

Janisha Patel (9)
St Michael's Primary School, Highgate

THE STARS

I can see the stars up in the sky,
Sparkling stars
they're not just ordinary stars.
I know that there's something
in them that I don't know about.
One of these stars is a special star
but I don't know which one.
The sparkling stars are all silvery
and if you're looking from the
sky it looks wonderful.
The special one is like
the leader of all the other stars.
It's quite dark, so you can only see
the light of the stars, nothing else.

Monika Krakowiak (9)
St Michael's Primary School, Highgate

ALIEN

What's up there in outer space?
Please will someone solve my case
How far are we from it? How far is it from us?
Why all the fuss?
The wind the sun
Do they have fun?
Do they throw a fit,
Do they punch and kick?
Do they love and care?
Are there aliens out there?

Katie Cumming (8)
St Michael's Primary School, Highgate

PERFECT UNIVERSE

You watch the sun bow her head in silent prayer,
She doesn't belong to you, nor me.
Being near her is like being near a heavy alarm,
You don't know what will set her off.
She closes her eyes and thinks of life and love,
In a perfect universe.
You watch a shooting star go past, your mind fixing on it.
Your insane mind fills itself with thoughts like water from a jug,
Thoughts about a perfect universe.
You're lost for words.
Someone is pulling you down but you're not going,
You'll stay with me and the sun in a perfect universe.
You don't need gravity,
Because you're free, free from that demon.
You're living with me and the sun,
In a perfect universe as a big family.
Pins and needles are sticking into me,
Are they sticking into you?
They're not are they?
You're perfect, perfect as harmony,
Perfect as the universe.

Cora Gilroy-Ware (10)
St Michael's Primary School, Highgate

THE SPACE JOURNEY

I am travelling up to space
and I can feel the cold air underneath me.
I can see big things like lollipops.
I am sweating to pieces in my boiling hot suit.
I am scared and I am wobbling like
a bird flapping its wings quickly.

Scarlett Smithson (9)
St Michael's Primary School, Highgate

COMETS

A cold, hard sphere runs across the sky
A fiery tail waving wildly around.
I could taste its heat, feel its hardness
Hear its wails and smell its smoke.
The sphere splits into a star burning like sand
on a tropical island.

The sphere does not mind the silvery, black sky slowly getting
darker than a hard lump of coal.
It did not seem to mind the brightness of the galaxy,
nor the warmth of the sun.
But every star it avoided, running and jumping down to Earth
until, with a sizzle and a crackle, the sphere just fell deeper
into the darkness.

Eleanor Harding (9)
St Michael's Primary School, Highgate

SPACE THOUGHTS

I swirl in the whirlpool of black oil,
Sinking into blank nothingness.
Catching glimpses of rainbow-coloured planets.
Drowning in its hugeness.
I, just a tiny pink speck in the whole of space.
An unintelligent being.
Only flesh and bone and pointless wondering.
We as humans think only of ourselves,
Our looks,
Our intelligence.
We are only wandering mists.

Rosie Dunnett (9)
St Michael's Primary School, Highgate

PLANETS

I'm the Earth.
I've got turf.
I've got toads.
I've got roads.
I'm Mars.
I'm near the stars.
I'm Jupiter.
People say I'm stupider
than any other planet.
But what about the sun?

I'm the sun, I'm the best.
Anyone that says I'm stupid
Is just a little pest.
Everyone orbit me
Because I've got sea.
But if I did
I'd be like a candle with a lid.
Everybody needs me, I'm simply the best
Everyone who says I'm not is just a little pest.

Everything apart from me is stupid and boring
But I'm the best
Better than the rest.

Jenny Law (8)
St Michael's Primary School, Highgate

THE UNIVERSE ELEPHANT

He landed on Venus
And bounced off Mars,
He raised his trunk to the moon and stars.
This animal belongs to another place
He belongs to outer space.
An infant in the solar system
learning from his father's wisdom.
The elephant goes were nobody goes,
Where earthquakes rumble and lava flows.
Sharpening his tusks among the red rocks,
The clouds look like wool from some purple socks.
His giant footsteps make the earth shake,
by a bubbling, boiling, steaming lake.

The land is bleak, the air is gas
The planet is a bubbling, boiling mass.
His ears are big, his tusks are sharp,
He blows his trunk with a loud *parp! Parp!*
His skin is blotched, his skin is red,
and by his age you'd think he was dead.
Down on Pluto in the dust,
The elephant sleeps (you know he must)!
On some distant moon or star,
He knows where other elephants are.
He went to wander (it was a curse)
So now he roams the universe.
Huge volcanoes erupting now
avalanches *pow! Pow! Pow!*
Giant spaceships shooting lasers,
fascinating old star gazers.
The elephant goes where nobody goes,
Where earthquakes rumble and lava flows.

Laurence Osborn (8)
St Michael's Primary School, Highgate

THE START

A speck of flame,
Gently swaying in space,
The speck of flame has too much fire,
Burning in its small body.

It starts to feel tired,
Then gets restless,
The speck of flame wants to give way,
But it doesn't know it's going to make the universe.

The clouds come and want to be the flame,
So they spin to get as hot as the flame,
Like ballerinas turning skilfully,
But they don't get as hot as the flame,
So some explode and others turn into worlds and drift away.

Rachael McKenzie (8)
St Michael's Primary School, Highgate

A TOUR OF SPACE

Shooting stars whizzing by,
Earth and Mars are in the sky.
Disappearing into space,
A dark and dreary place.
Until you meet the sun that is,
The biggest star of all.
The little stars do their best to keep up with the rest,
The shattering brightness blinds me.
The darkness is so dim,
So I've made up my mind, I'm staying in!

Diane Shaw (9)
St Michael's Primary School, Highgate

SKYLIGHT SCENE

I looked through the opening,
A skylight, a window to the stars.
I saw dark bliss.
Peacefulness.

Drifting stars,
Lonely, yet surrounded in a black throbbing mass.
Like shining jewels,
Illuminating the night sky.

The fiery shadows of other planets,
Doused in cool moonlight.
Their pale reflections showing
Through the timeless warp.

Nicholas Rawlinson (10)
St Michael's Primary School, Highgate

THE STARS

The magical bright stars,
Flashing around the sky,
Floating high above all humans
A small light in the dark night.
The great planets stand beside the bright stars.
Stars are happy to me
Lighting up the night sky
No matter where you are you'll see a star.

Jonathan Spencer (10)
St Michael's Primary School, Highgate

SPACE

Space is a sea of death.
Bodies washed ashore as quickly
as dinosaurs were wiped out.
A hell of sadness and loneliness
a well of souls scattered
carelessly across the universe.
Like water in the sea
a well of life
a still death
a whale plunging
down like a life
fading away.
An eclipse of colour
a bright new start
a new life
a second chance
a trust
a friend
a bird with new wings.

Harry Walton (9)
St Michael's Primary School, Highgate

BLACK HOLE

The suffering roof of black
Letting nothing escape its tremendous grasp.
It was as vivid as the picture in my mind
Sucking everything within its reach.
Taking my soul and scarring my life.

Luke French (10)
St Michael's Primary School, Highgate

ALIEN ATTACK

Spaceship flying
Mars ahead!
Creatures around, not people
Stench of decaying flesh
Aliens, the dreaded *Borg!*
Destruction and death.

Spaceship flying
Return to Earth
Creatures around not people.
Leader of *Borg* running this way.

Fear
I look up
I see nothing, no moon, no stars, no Mars, nothing
All I see is the *Borg* ship
Destruction and *Death.*

Laura Bell (10)
St Michael's Primary School, Highgate

MAYBE

Is the Moon of green cheese?
Or is it a strong white light bulb hanging from space?
It might be an enlarged fossil or half of planet Jupiter
Could it be a see-through bottle top stuck on to the Sun?
Maybe it is just a mass of rock,
How disappointing.

Emma Whitehead (10)
St Michael's Primary School, Highgate

THE SHINING SKY

As I look through the unknown sky,
nothing's there,
I walk away like tipping my life
at an angle.
Then something touched me, I fell on a blanket
of the smoothest silk bed.
It was like an arrow had just
gone through me.
A glittering golden eye fell upon me.
It felt like a shimmering heat
was nearby.
I looked behind me it was like
love had touched me.
My mind dropped then my heart fell.

Emily Doyle (9)
St Michael's Primary School, Highgate

STARS

Stars are a beautiful silver
Like candles lighting up the dark.
The warmth of a glow of happiness
The cold of crystal-white ice.
A choir of angels singing
A fire of blazing heat.
A dazzling sight that you can't beat
Twinkling silently in the dark night sky.

Sophie Lake (10)
St Michael's Primary School, Highgate

PALACE COSMOS

The universe is a palace,
With servants here and there,
With gauzy yellow dresses,
And glitzy yellow hair.

A black hole is a demon lord,
A white hole is a king,
Who brings evil in from one end,
From the other, good comes out from within.

The universe is a palace,
Which, in our minds, is oversize.
But for beings of a planet's kind,
It's a glory for the eyes.

Catherine Goy (10)
St Michael's Primary School, Highgate

THE ONGOING CYCLE

Stars shining brilliant and true,
Never does one stop,
to guard the moon and earth.
If one breaks from the cycle,
the rings of space and eternity,
the earth shall be crushed,
by stars, shining true.

Max Wakefield (10)
St Michael's Primary School, Highgate

THE GOLDEN LION

The lion shakes his mane and pushes
the silver moon away,
Ready to start a new beginning for the day.
He shines on the people, houses and trees,
He shines on the rivers, oceans and seas.
He shines on the runner as he quickens his pace,
He shines in every single place.
And now the moon comes into view,
And now up come the fire-sparks, too.
As moon stays there when no human is awake,
And lion appears at daybreak.

Grace Durham (9)
St Michael's Primary School, Highgate

SPACE

Opening the gap
made for us to look into.
To take out that chance
relying on our strengths
and our thoughts
that find out
what it holds for our future
and what it holds for yours.

Maximilian Bryant (9)
St Michael's Primary School, Highgate,

SPACE IS A DREAM

As I gaze up in the air,
I see dark red dragons dancing gracefully,
Blowing sparkles of fire everywhere.
It is like broken hearts going mad in anger.
My mind is going crazy as it looks into space.
The black, foggy mist has gone,
A crack of an egg has formed
And the lion's mane appears.
For the night has disappeared and morning has come.
Like a flower opening its first few buds.
The night is truly over and the sun has arrived
Like it's ringing on the doorbell.
For it has lost something that is its partner the night.

Phoebe Fisher (9)
St Michael's Primary School, Highgate

STARS

A circle of snowdrops suddenly falling,
One flower is left with light,
like a diamond and silver ring.

A black waterfall covers this star,
but though I feel my heart is sinking
The true star still shines on.

Camilla MacSwiney (8)
St Michael's Primary School, Highgate

STARS

The stars ride on their silver soft horse's back.
They hurt the night with their wisdom
They don't let night enslave them.
They enter the tunnel of truth and don't get rejected.

They lay every night showing the banner of truth
They give us the light of birth.
As I look up at the star I hear their dream like Martin Luther King.

The stars show light but death gives night
Death takes light like a paralysed sheep.
Death wears a black cloak flying through the orbit
reading astrology.

Rochelle Williams (9)
St Michael's Primary School, Highgate

STARS

I can see a white crystal ball.
Hot stars burning away,
until they form into shooting stars.
Shooting stars are like doves,
flying to the top of the world,
and never coming back,
until the world ends.

Sophie Durant-Aref (9)
St Michael's Primary School, Highgate

THE COSMIC CALENDAR

January is Uranus
Bleak and biting cold

February is Venus
The month when love unfolds.

March is for Mars
When fighting men are bold.

April is for Neptune
April showers behold.

May is the Milky Way
A splatter of cosmic mould.

June is for Saturn
The wedding rings of gold.

July is Jupiter
King of summer I'm told.

August is the Sun
When strong heat can scald.

September is for Comets
Across the sky unrolled.

October is for Moon
The planets' friend of old.

November is for Mercury
A messenger taking the untold.

December is Pluto
The underworld where life's on hold.

Winifred Herbstein (8)
St Michael's Primary School, Highgate

SPACE IS A DIFFERENT PLACE

In the night the stars come out
shining like light bulbs in a house.
But up in space it's a different tale
the sun is shining day and night.
Space is a different world, a different place
the stars are called meteors burning bits of rock.
In space some planets are unknown
like Venus, Jupiter and Mars.
Rockets tried to get there but didn't get that far
who knows if we ever get there!
Because I can't tell.

Julian Barnes
St Michael's Primary School, Highgate

CONSTELLATION

I spy my constellation on the new chart.
Getting gently into dust on the floor.
Like a soft, sharp snowflake sensing the ground.
Freezing out the devil's truth of wisdom.
Like a volcano erupting
And I live no more.

Joshua Hogan (8)
St Michael's Primary School, Highgate

THE BLACK HOLE

Bang!
The star explodes
Blackness,
       Darkness
So much energy,
Not even light can escape
Now it is a black hole.
Never to be seen again . . .
       I think.

Imogen Whittam (9)
St Michael's Primary School, Highgate

I KNOW A PERSON

I know a person who's
adventurous, cunning and quite fast.
He's a goody-goody. Oh what!
He's a pain in the butt!
He never cleans his room it looks like
a jungle there!
And he leaves his homework till the last day!
He hardly shuts up in class!
He never lies , ok only a little!
Oh! Should I have told you that, because
That's me!

Adam Whitty (9)
St Monica's RC Primary School

CAR JOURNEY

I'm on my way to the airport,
I'm going to Timbuktu.
I've been driving for hours,
Oh Mum I need the loo.
'Are we there yet?' I said,
'No dear but nearly.'
Twenty minutes later . . .
'Are we there yet?' I said,
'No dear but nearly.'
Forty minutes later . . .
'Are we there yet?' I said
'No dear but nearly.'
One hour later . . .
'Are we there yet?' I said
'No dear but nearly.'
'How long is nearly?' I said angrily
'Oh only three hours longer
So sit quietly.'

Daniel Monsurate (8)
St Monica's RC Primary School

CAR WASHES

I am always scared going into car washes.
I say to my mum, 'Put me in the boot,'
She replies 'Don't be silly it's just a car wash.'
I am scared of those blue prickly things,
they are going to attack me.
I will just hide my face under my jacket,
I feel relieved when the car wash is over.

Sean O'Mahony (9)
St Monica's RC Primary School

THE SKY IS FALLING

I'm reading a boring, in fact a very boring, book
My mum gives me a look.
'Ok' I said I picked up the book.
I read 'The sky is
falling oh hurry up Foxy Loxy'! . . . 'Mum' I shouted.

'Yes' mum's making a cup of tea,
I can think better when mum's not nagging me.
I ran upstairs and hid under the bed
'I hope mum won't find me.' I whispered to Ted.
Bad luck she has!

'What are you doing under the bed?' sighed mum.
'The sky's falling, so I'm under the bed!'
'Oh don't be silly' mum said.
'It is, it is,' I cried with glee
'Come and see, come and see.'
We stood at the window looking out.
The clouds were falling all about.
'Good Lord' said mum peeping out
'We'd better get the umbrellas out!'

Anna Reynolds (8)
St Monica's RC Primary School

TEACHERS

I go out to the playground
and what do I see?
A teacher in the staff room
drinking a cup of tea.
I see a teacher telling Ciara off.
Why don't they tell me off for a change?

Lisa Delaney (8)
St Monica's RC Primary School

WHY IS MY CAT FAT?

Why is my cat so fat?
Is it because he sits on my lap
Or is it because he eats
Too many sweets
Oh why my cat?

Why is my cat so fat?
Is it because he eats too much fish
Or is it because he eats from a dish
Oh why my cat?

Is my cat fat
because I always give him food
when they say he's never rude.
                    Oh no!

Amanda Nartey (8)
St Monica's RC Primary School

ANIMALS

It is quite amazing,
when cockerels crow,
and how the glow worms seem to glow.
But the animal that amazes me most,
is the tiger, as strong, as a post.
The pigs tend to boast,
I don't really like them the most.
The leopards have their spots,
and the chickens, have their feathers,
but they still go out,
whatever the type of weather.

Claudia Haussmann (9)
St Monica's RC Primary School

I DREAMT

I dreamt that I was a full moon
Shining by the stars.
I dreamt that I was a star
Twinkling in the night.
I dreamt that I was a wish
Wishing for a thousand wishes
that would be commanded.
Though I never thought that,
When you dream you are day-dreaming.
That you are a dream
Even though you can't see a dream
It exists in your heart forever.

Saffienne Vincent (8)
St Monica's RC Primary School

I WONDER

I wonder why the grass is green
and why the wind is never seen.
Who taught the birds to build their nests,
and why the trees have a rest.
I wonder why our brain is grey,
and why people are named Ray.
I wonder why the snow is white,
and how we learn wrong from right.
I wonder why the grass is green,
and why the wind is never seen.

Joseph McCormack (9)
St Monica's RC Primary School

THE WORLD I NEVER KNEW

Teddy bear's dressed
in a coat of brown fur.
The speedy hare with
a big bag of myrrh.
A snail carrying
the king on his back,
Or maybe a tortoise having a snack.
Purple apples on a few trees
people swimming in pink seas.
Animals eating, pencils for tea,
Or even my fish talking to me.
Felt-tips colouring by themselves,
paint boxes spinning on multicoloured shelves.
They have sandwiches full of salt and pepper,
full of relish and mayonnaise, full of ketchup and butter.
It goes all the way past their gutters.
It really is sickening how could they stay alive,
I really can't believe that I am believing it.

Clare Bagland (9)
St Monica's RC Primary School